In my new Liverpool home

By James Hamilton

Dedicated to the Rev Norman Meeten and his wife Jenny who's life and work has been instrumental in so many lives here in Liverpool, the UK and throughout the world

Foreword

Continuing from the previous two books of our life story written by me and my sister Grace, this new part is essentially the story of my life after coming to Liverpool, where, to my surprise, I ended up staying.

It's quite a few years ago now since my wife Jean and I went down to the Midlands to attend a family funeral. Afterwards we gathered in the home of one of my cousins for refreshments. As we stood around chatting, an elderly uncle who was very deaf said loudly, 'Don't ever grow old Jimmy, it's a right ******."

The room was now silent as everyone looked at him in shock and then in my direction. It didn't bother me though; after all, I had been in farming myself and knew all the language that was common in those circles.

Then 'Are you still religious, Jimmy?' he boomed. I thought for a few seconds, trying to find the right answer to that one, but in the end plumbed for the easy reply, 'Yes'.

It wasn't the right time then to give a fuller explanation of how I had been religious in my younger days when I had gone to church fairly regularly with my mum, but at the age of 19 I had a spiritual experience that changed my life. This book is an attempt to give an account of what it has meant to me over the last 50 years to be a Christian.

It's been such a great adventure and a rich experience not to be missed!

This account starts fifty years ago and these are the

memories which have remained with me. Others who read this might remember other things or maybe a different version.

I kept diaries of these years, admittedly not with a lot of detail but at least I have dates and places to remind me of happenings.

I am so thankful to God for allowing me to be in Liverpool at this time and to have a small part in all that happened at the Devonshire Road Christian Fellowship.

There were lots of other things that happened around this time involving others in the church which I will try to mention but I may not be totally accurate. Maybe others will follow on and write their own memories eventually.

Amazing grace! How sweet the sound
That saved a wretch like me!
I once was lost, but now am found;
Was blind, but now I see.

'Twas grace that taught my heart to fear,
And grace my fears relieved;
How precious did that grace appear
The hour I first believed.

Through many dangers, toils, and snares,
I have already come;
'Tis grace hath brought me safe thus far,
And grace will lead me home.

John Newton 1725-1807

Table of Contents

Foreword	3
Chapter 1: Arriving in Liverpool	7
THE BEGINNINGS OF 137 QUEENS ROAD.	
John's Time at Devy Road	
Fred's story	
Chapter 2: Settling into my new work	24
Chapter 3: Four just men	39
Chapter 4: Further trips to Italy 1972	50
Chapter 5: A significant year – 1973	63
Chapter 6: Jean Thorpe	73
Chapter 7: 1974: My final trip to Italy	80
Chapter 8: My time working in the house comes to an end: 1974	90
Chapter 9: Marriage – the early years	104
Lancashire Electric Lamp	
Our trials at home	
Chapter 10: 1976: Glad times and sad times	123
Chapter 11: Parenthood and moving forward	131
Chapter 12: James Hamilton, Painter and Decorator	138
Chapter 13: Neighbours and friends	144
Chapter 14: Northern Italy earthquake	151
Chapter 15: Bryn Goleu, Lanfairfechan	181

Chapter 1: Arriving in Liverpool

In our previous book, my sister Grace and I wrote about our childhood, starting with our life in Scotland where we were born, and then about our move to Birmingham after the death of our father when I was nine. We lived with our mother in a small cottage on the edge of Birmingham, just inside Worcestershire. It was very different from the life we had experienced in Scotland but after a while we managed to adjust, acquired English accents and fitted in with our new life.

We finished our schooling and got jobs as soon as we were allowed, which made a big difference for us financially as a family. I left school with no qualifications and had only one job I wanted to do; I had been helping out on my uncle Arthur's farm in the summer and at weekends and could think of nothing better I would like to do.

Thankfully, my uncle agreed to take me on and I thought I would make farming my career. After a few years however I felt there was something missing in the life I was living, and I started off on a search for the meaning of life. At the age of 19 I found out what it was. I gave my life to Christ and it changed everything for me. God now became real to me, like a father in heaven that cared for me, who I could pray to and know He heard and answered my prayers, sometimes in quite amazing and surprising ways. Although I loved the farming life, I felt God had other plans for me, so I left and over the next four years I had various jobs and took part in two mission trips to Italy.

At the age of 23, I came up to Liverpool to a church fellowship we'd previously visited on a number of occasions for the conferences that were held every year. I thought I was coming for a couple of months or so to reflect and consider my present and future life, but as it turned out, my "short time" away from home turned out to be nine months, during which I began to feel quite at home, both in Liverpool and in the church house where I now lived.

That is where book 2 ended, and this is the continuation of the story. It is where my account diverges from Grace's. She remained in Birmingham and I ended up finding Liverpool was my new permanent home. From here on, this is essentially the story of my life and experiences although I may include accounts of others from time to time to fill in the gaps.

In April 1970 I came to Liverpool with a small suitcase. Paul and Mary (friends from church) brought me in their Land-Rover (which broke down on the way), but we still got there in the end somehow. I had given up my job in a medical warehouse to come to stay in Liverpool and join the church known as the Devonshire Road Christian Fellowship.

On my last day of work I had received a letter from the Rev Norman Meeten who was the founder of this new church, advising me that I would be welcome to come and stay for a short while in the house and to find a job for the time I would be there.

To get an understanding of this church fellowship, the following article was included in a blog on the Devonshire Road Christian Fellowship website: it is a copy of the first newsletter written by Norman Meeten giving an account of how the work in Liverpool began.

THE BEGINNINGS OF 137 QUEENS ROAD.

The existence of the work at 137 Queens Road is simply the answer to prayer. At the beginning of September 1964, I left St. Saviour, Falkner Square, and withdrew from parish work in obedience to the Lord. I went home to Sussex not knowing what the Lord would have me do next. My heart was still much drawn to Liverpool. Within a month I found myself back in the North at The Longcroft, Barnston, Cheshire. I stayed there and helped with the work in a small way, and at the same time sought the Lord regarding the future. While at the Longcroft it became quite apparent, from the demands for ministry in Liverpool that if these demands were to be met, a centre was essential in the city. At the end of November, we were offered an eleven roomed house for a rent of £3. 5. 0. p.w. in Queen's Road Liverpool 6, a district with the highest delinquent rate in the City. Mrs J. Porter and I viewed the property – prayed earnestly concerning it – believed it to be the answer to our prayers – and took it.

Structurally the house was in good condition but owing to neglect, the interior was in a sad state of decay. We set to work almost immediately but owing to the sudden death of my father the work was suspended until the New Year. Within six weeks, with the help of a grand band of young people, the complete house was put in order and decorated, from attic to basement. The work was hard but the fellowship was great. There was much spiritual blessing and unity. Praise God! From the very first day the spiritual side of the work has had first priority. Much praying was done midst the painting and cleaning. Numbers of people sought for ministry in those days and were blessed. The first room to be completed was the largest room in the house – the front room on the first floor – which is the fellowship room. Here we meet regularly for worship and fellowship, and twice a week we have a Bible Study, when Mr. North, Overseer of the Longcroft, usually ministers. The House seem to be very much like an Inn between earth and heaven. There is a continual flow of people from all walks of life and more and more from all parts of the world. My prayer is that it may continually be a Bethel – a place where man and God meet.

There is more content by Norman about the beginnings of the Devonshire Road Christian Fellowship Website for those interested - www.devyroad.com

After a while, this terraced house became too small and a bigger one was sought. Eventually a large house on Devonshire Road, Toxteth came to their attention. It was in a terribly rundown state but was ideal for their needs and was eventually bought for the amazing price of £2000, just half the asking price. The work of restoring it to its former glory then began in earnest as the folk in the fellowship converted the building to meet the needs of the church. This work continued for many years and was still on-going when I came to live there.

On arriving in Liverpool, I managed to get a job straight away in Plessey's, a factory producing telephone equipment, where I remained for nine months. It was pretty repetitive work but it was made more interesting with the Liverpool banter which went on every day with the Scouse lads round the workbench.

Life in the church house was quite a bit different from anything I had experienced before. My nine months was a very lovely experience, living in a place where I had great friendships with the folk in the house and I made many friends in the church fellowship, which must have numbered more than two hundred at that time, many of them young people of about my age.

The fellowship had already become quite well known in Liverpool before I joined it and was attracting quite a few visitors. Of course, there were a number of good churches in the area at that time but in my view, the Devonshire Road Fellowship made its mark for several reasons. It was started by a respected C of E curate who had a desire to know God in a deeper way and wanted to help others to know and love this wonderful God also. The resultant meetings were quite different from what I had ever known before. In my previous experience, church had tended to be more formal, led from the front with often a rather intellectual sermon. The leaders of this new church made the meeting much more informal, open for church members to participate in choosing hymns and songs as the service proceeded, and for individuals to pray spontaneously or give a short word or testimony. Usually, one of the leaders would complete the time with preaching from the scriptures, sometimes prepared earlier, but at other times developing some of the themes that had emerged during the meeting.

There were many local people in the fellowship, but there were also some young people who had come to Liverpool University or other local colleges and had heard of the church. After being part of the church during their studies some decided to stay on in Liverpool to be a part of it. I think it's true to say that many friendships started at that time and remain strong to this day, even though most people have moved on to other parts of the country and even around the world. One of the lads, Brett, was from Birmingham like me; we ended up sharing a bedroom and he became my best friend, in fact he was my Best Man when I eventually got married and I was his at his wedding.

Initially, I shared a bedroom on the middle floor of the large Victorian house with four other lads who were about my age. There were some full-time workers who also lived in the house – Ken Whiteway, who managed much of the office work, and Dave Wetherley, a carpenter. Dave was also one of the leaders in the church, who were known as elders. He had a young man working with him, Peter Gray, and between them they did much of the practical work of renovating the house, which at this stage was still very much a work in progress. There were also two girls who lived in the top flat in no.16, the house next door which was rented; they did all the housekeeping and cooking down in the basement of the church house, no.14. Norman and his wife Jenny lived on the top floor of no.14, having moved in after they married.

In the basement dining room, there was a beautiful mahogany table which could seat about 16 people – it must have been about 20 ft long! The girls who worked in the house over the years did such a wonderful job catering for all the people who lived there as well as for the constant flow of visitors.

A rather poor photo of lunch in the dining room, 1971

I found myself in a very different life than previously, and there were many things I had to get used to that I had not experienced at home in Birmingham. For one thing we'd never had a phone at home so I quickly had to get used to answering it here.

The phone would ring many times through the day, and whoever was nearest it was expected to answer with the correct phrase, 'Hello, 14 Devonshire Road.' The next thing was to find the person who was wanted, who more often than not would be Norman on the top floor. This was before the days of modern technology, so one had to run up three flights of stairs to announce breathlessly there was a call for him and he could then answer it on his extension. After a few months of this I thought I really had to do something about it. I found a shop in the city that sold intercom systems and set about wiring it up to all the different flats. Jeff Clapham, one of the other lads residing in the house at the time, has never let me forget that I had wires trailing everywhere through both the houses. Unfortunately, in the process of connecting to the top flat next door (the girls' flat), I put a cable clip through the phone cable belonging to the elderly lady in the middle flat and she had to call out the GPO engineers to sort it out. Fortunately, she didn't seem to be too upset!

The house team when I started work there.

One other thing was new to me: I had to do my own washing at the local launderette and then the ironing, which Mum had always done for me back home. Sometimes though, one of the girls would offer to do it for me, which of course I would gratefully accept.

After a few months of living in the house I discovered that Lesley and Sheila who were in charge of the kitchens took the house laundry, i.e. sheets, towels and so on, to the local wash house which was still operating at that time, and as it was on my way home from work, I started dropping in on them to lend a hand.

What an interesting place it was! There were huge washing machines, spin dryers, big tubs for smaller items which you stirred with a paddle and finally the drying racks upstairs where you hung your washing – because it was so hot up there it was all dry within minutes. It was very humid work though and by the end of it we would all would return home with glowing red faces. There was a missionary called Jackie Jackson who was back from Brazil staying with us for a while. She used to help with this task and her comment was that it was hotter than being in the jungle!

During these months, I was still returning home regularly to see Mum. Grace was still living at home with her, but I felt a responsibility to see she was all right until I went to live back home, as I expected to do. We had managed to get our old VW Beetle going again and it faithfully took me on those trips up and down the M6 at 60 miles an hour. You could hear the bearings in the engine rattling away but it still kept going somehow.

Grace's fiancée returned from India later that year and they got married on 17th October 1970 on a pleasant sunny day. I had the privilege of taking her down the aisle. The little cottage next to Mum's was vacant so they moved in and lived there till they managed to buy a house, still very close to her.

Toward the end of the year, I returned to Liverpool from a weekend at Mum's with the feeling that Birmingham was no longer my home. I was quite emotional at the thought and wondered what was going to happen next.

That December, as I considered my position, I felt I had three possible options. I'd heard of a Christian bookshop in Kendal that needed an assistant (not that I knew anything about selling books!). Then there was a friend from Birmingham (Clive Colwell) who had gone to Glasgow Bible College a few years earlier and was now involved with a church in Glasgow working on the streets with alcoholics and drug addicts. As I quite fancied living in Scotland again, I thought I could go and join him in the work. The third option I considered was to offer to work in the church house where I was already, in Liverpool. In my 1970 diary I see that I shared these thoughts just before Christmas with the elders of the church. It records that they agreed they would like me to come and work in the house 'for a short time'.

That Christmas, Norman and Jenny invited all the people living in the fellowship house up to their flat for Christmas dinner (there were several folk staying there then). This was typical of the attention and love they gave to all who came to the house or stayed there for whatever reason or need they had in their lives.

Following this, there were some changes in the household. Norman had been asked by the Longcroft fellowship, which met in a big house out in the Wirral countryside, if he and Jenny would come over to lead the work there, starting in early 1971. As well as this, one of the other leaders, Dick Hussey, was going with his wife Sylvia to join a work in Spain. It was decided by the elders of the Devonshire Road fellowship to appoint two new elders to take up the work. After much deliberation and prayer, two of the young men in the church were commissioned to the eldership (in late 1970, I think): John Valentine, who was a salesman for a big woodchip firm, and Fred Tomlinson who with his wife Sheila and three children had already given up his home to live in the ground floor flat next door at no.16 and had taken on the administration of the work.

John had been in the church for some time, but I hadn't really got to know him until he moved into the top flat with us at that point. Here is his part of the story:

John's Time at Devy Road

I was one of those who moved from Queens Road to No.14. I had a full-time job then, but all our free time and efforts were spent on work parties. My first job in the house was to help clear the basement. It had been used as a rubbish tip and took about 2 months to clean out all the muck and filth. In the meantime, others worked on different rooms. I moved into the house and Mr North suggested that the meeting room was not big enough, so we decided to knock down a wall. At the time I was working for a timber firm and was the liaison rep with the City Engineering Department. In passing, I mentioned to the town engineer that we were knocking down a wall. He said we needed planning permission and approval from the City Engineer but he agreed to come round and advise us. A good thing he did! He told us the basement walls would not carry the weight of the necessary steel beam (an RSJ) and we needed to build an extra wall there. When the wall was knocked down and the RSJ put across, Dave Wetherley went upstairs only to find the doors wouldn't open as the floor was sinking. He hurriedly rushed down and stuffed slates on top of the beam to prevent more subsidence. We were ignorant but God was gracious….

In 1970 or 71, I was ordained an elder with Fred Tomlinson. I shared a flat with Brett Wolfindale, Jim Hamilton, Dave Wetherley and, over time, many others.

Fred Tomlinson, who was also made an elder at this time (he's now a pastor in Canada), was asked for his part in the story.

Fred's story

A series of events came about, all converging in our move into 14 Devonshire Road. I was in the Liverpool Police Force and it was my 'dream' career; it was just beginning to open up to me. One day when I was on a police operation, I was stabbed in the back. The Chief of Police was standing not far from me and witnessed it, and in the words of my Chief Inspector, it was the best thing that could have happened. He told me that any application from me going across his desk was certain to be accepted!

However, just then I went to Queens Road where the fellowship first started and God met me, and my world was turned up-side-down. Just a few short steps from applying for a transfer to Traffic police, I felt led by the Lord to resign. I have often wondered if I had remained in the police force, how my life would have turned out if I had moved on with Traffic police.

That decision was a very big one. I remember talking to Pastor North and saying, "I have a real problem, I was so certain that the Lord had opened the way for me to join the police." He said, "There's no problem!! God led you in, now He's leading you out!"

My Chief called me a fool. A visit to Mr and Mrs North, who were living now in Exeter, was another milestone. There's a story here, but to be brief, something he said was the trigger for us to sell our house in Ashton in Makerfield. The goal was to unload the mortgage we had, another big (and crazy) change. We then moved into the rented 'cockroach house' at Queens Road – another crazy move!

Driving from there to Devy Road for the Sunday morning meeting, I felt the Lord tell me I was to sell our car and pay off the loan on the house. Seated in the meeting before it started, Keith Kelly, who was sitting behind me, said, "I don't suppose you're interested in selling your car are you?" I said, "Keith, you won't believe this...."

"How much to you want for it?" he asked. I told him what I owed on the mortgage and he said, "Let's do some Christian bargaining." He then offered me more than I needed... Keith and Phil Williamson were going to visit missionaries on the continent and had decided they wanted to buy the same kind of car that I owned. Amazing!

When a Christian man, one of the directors at Blakes, my previous employer, heard I had left the police, he contacted me and asked if I would be interested in having lunch with him. I did and he offered me a post back in the company to develop their printing department, which I took.

A couple of years later, I attended a church business meeting, in which we were told that in the light of Norman's developing ministry, it was obvious that someone else should move into the house as an administrator. That information went in one ear and out of the other. A week later I was operating a printing machine, when right out of the blue, I believe I heard the Lord speak to me and say, "You and Sheila are the couple to move into the House." I was so shocked, I immediately stopped the machine and sat down, stunned. That night I shared this with Sheila and later visited Norman. His response was, "Well it could be, I will share this with the elders." They were all in favour and a business meeting was arranged. We were excluded from the meeting while a vote was taken. Later, we were told it was unanimous with just one exception – my auntie Daisy!

So immediately before the Cliff Conference Week in August 1970, we moved into the flea-ridden ground floor flat in 16 Devonshire Road. We were the first occupants in that then rented flat. The plan was that as soon as Norman was able to get relocated to the Longcroft, we would move into 14.

In retelling this story, I have always been reminded of the words of Jim Elliot, a missionary to a primitive tribe in Ecuador: "How blind we would have been to have missed the Lord's leading in the early days." Praise the Lord! Another saying of his which has meant much to me through my life is "He is no fool, who gives what he cannot keep, to gain what he cannot lose."

****

Now, returning to my own story... I went home to spend Christmas 1970 with Mum in Birmingham, and on my return to Liverpool in the new year, went to see my boss and handed in my notice. He was also a Christian and an elder in a Brethren church. He was happy to receive my notice until he asked what I was going to do and what the pay would be. When I explained that, like the others working in the fellowship house, I would have to trust God to provide for my needs, and I would be getting only my bed and board, he was most concerned about this and thought, like Fred's boss, that I was crazy.

I never met him again after I left so was unable to tell him how I lacked for nothing in the next four years while I lived and worked in the house. Indeed, I had many experiences of my needs being met, often in quite remarkable ways, and although I thought I was going to be doing mostly practical work in the house, it turned out to be much more than I was expecting. What actually happened was quite life changing for me and I had so many adventures!

My diary tells me I finished work at Plessey's on Friday 5th January 1971 and started at the house on the following Monday. Having lived there for nine months and helped out in various ways, it seemed quite natural to be part of the work force. I think the difference for me now was that there seemed to be no particular pattern or schedule to my days. There was plenty of painting and decorating to get on with, but every day was full of various challenges and other things that suddenly took priority.

Each day began with breakfast round the big table in the basement with all the workers from 8 till 9 o'clock. After washing up, everyone got on with the jobs of the day. I got into a routine of dropping in on Fred and Sheila in the middle flat to see if there was anything they needed me to do. They had their breakfast there with their family of three young children and would inevitably ask me if I would like a cup of tea and a slice of toast and jam while we talked – a nice second breakfast!

Every day was varied. I might have an idea of what I wanted to accomplish but often other things would supersede my plan and the day would turn out different. However, because I was working as part of a team, it was always a pleasure to get on with it.

All the workers in the house worked a six-day week with one day off. Days off were staggered to ensure that there was always someone on duty – there could be visitors, calls for help, enquiries, requests for counselling or many other needs unexpectedly occurring day and night. Also, we ran a kids' club on Friday nights, which meant we got to know lots of the children in the district, some of whom were difficult characters and would sometimes come and cause us trouble. All in all, each day tended to be busy and believe me, you were glad to have a day off!

When I had time off, I often found it best to go out for the day, in that way I wouldn't get involved with the busy-ness of the house. Quite often I would go over to the Wirral and spend the day at the Longcroft, where there was a nice library where I could sit and quietly read and perhaps have a bit of a snooze. The folk there were always glad to have me over when I needed a rest. Once I got so tired that I had a carbuncle on my neck and a nurse who was part of the fellowship there insisted on tending it for me and told me to stay for a few days' rest till it was better.It was a lot of fun for us lads living together in the top flat of the house. Quite often last thing at night John, Dave, Brett and myself would end up in the rather small kitchen making our hot chocolate and maybe toast, many times talking and laughing over the things we had been doing. On Sundays, we always dressed smartly for our church services, (notice the flashy tie which many of the lads wore in those days).

This is how we looked when we took our took turns on door duty welcoming people as they arrived.

Chapter 2: Settling into my new work

Up till this time, I had been using our old VW Beetle which was getting very tired. When John Miles returned from India and married Grace, they used the VW Caravanette, which had been out of action for a while till between us we got it fixed. John and Grace used it for a short time but then they bought a better car, so I brought it up to Liverpool. I think I can safely say it became very useful both for me and for the fellowship in many ways. It was pretty old by this time and the bodywork was rotting badly, but I set to and filled all the holes and hand-painted it with a white top and blue bottom. I think I did quite a good job! The photos shows my Mark One VW caravanette and Pete Moffat's Zephyr Zodiac.

When Fred and his family moved into the middle flat at no.14, we fellows moved to the top floor. I now shared a room with my friend Brett at the back of the house, Dave Wetherley and Peter Gray had bedrooms at the front, and John Valentine moved into a large bedroom at the back which also doubled up as his office. John was the son of a docker and was a successful salesman for a big firm that produced chipboard of all kinds. I would sometimes overhear him on the phone to customers saying that he could offer them so many million square feet at a very good price! I believe he was a very good salesman.

In my first week as a worker in no.14, a gentleman in a smart suit turned up for the Sunday service and afterwards I got into conversation with him. He was a missionary in Italy and, as I had been in Italy a couple of times on missions not too long before, we found we had a lot in common and got on really well. He had been visiting a church in Ireland who had heard of the Devonshire Road fellowship – some good things and some strange rumours as well – so he decided he to come and see for himself what was going on. It's true to say that the fellowship became well known in the 70s and some people came from quite a distance for services; one family came from Stafford every Sunday and later, another elderly couple came down from Blackpool every week.

I offered to show this visitor, Philip Wiles, around the house and he found it very interesting. At the end before leaving he asked if I would arrange for him to meet the elders of the church on the following day.

Next day he explained that the church he was connected with in Udine, Northern Italy had what they considered to be a problem. There was a young single girl in the group who was having a baby and they felt to save her shame it would be good if she could go away for a while until the baby was born. Would the Liverpool fellowship be prepared to have her and her mother come to stay? The elders agreed they would be welcome, so on 9th February 1971 Daniela and her mother Pierina arrived and were given accommodation in the ground floor flat in no.16. They spoke no English but fortunately one of the fellowship girls was fluent in Italian and I spoke a little, so we helped them to settle in and soon they were part of the family and much loved in the church.

Towards the end of March, I took Daniela and Mama in my caravanette to the Women's Hospital in Oxford Street where she was to have her baby. I was so nervous en route that I kept looking back to see she was all right and went through a red traffic light – I had to reverse quickly back over the line! Many years later Daniela said she remembered this and had found it very amusing. Anyway, I managed to get them there safely, and on the 25th March a lovely baby girl, Sara, was born.

During the year they stayed in Liverpool, I visited them from time to time in the evenings to try to help with their English, and found my Italian improved a little too. People in the fellowship were very kind to them, taking them out on trips to various places in the UK, Wales, the Lake District and even Scotland.

Around this time, Fred's brother Dave and his wife Pat, who also had been living with their children for a time in the church house, moved to Ripon to start a church fellowship, and Ken Whiteway went to Yorkshire to join them. Dave had been a powerful preacher in the church in those early days. I still remember him speaking from 2 Peter 1v19: "the day dawns and the morning star rises in our hearts."

Over the next few years, I visited Dave and Pat quite a few times. I think I helped them a bit initially with some decorating in their new home, but after that I enjoyed just going to see them and the church folk there – the Ripon area is a beautiful place to live and visit.

I remember going over once with Fred. Dave's car had broken down; it was a big old Rover, something like this one.

Fred kindly offered to swap cars with him and we brought his back to Liverpool to see if we could get it fixed. We went over in my VW van and towed Dave's car (steered by Fred) all the way back to Liverpool. The M62 was still under construction on the moors, so we travelled on the old winding roads across the Pennines. It would normally have been a very pleasant route, but it was no easy feat; when we finally got home, Fred said he had never had such a scary drive – he'd had to steer all the way without being able to see through the van to the road ahead.

I don't remember if the car ever got repaired. There was a small garage locally that we all used to go to when our cars needed fixing. Fred had found it and a man called Arthur Cook, who ran it, became a very good friend and started coming to some of the meetings with his wife. He sincerely wanted to do anything he could for Fred and his friends. The only trouble was that Arthur was not the best or most reliable mechanic you could meet. He also tended to offer the same solution for every car problem you went in with. The first thing he'd do was change the high-tension cables to the spark plugs, saying that this would fix it. Eventually he got the nickname "Arthur (high- tension-lead) Cook."

I had many other experiences of having to help rescue

people with broken-down cars in those days; I guess it was due to cars being less reliable then – and none of us could afford to be in the RAC. However, I won't bore you with all the stories – just one more…

We had a Nigerian pastor come on a visit and he wanted to go up to the Keswick Convention, so Fred and John Val agreed to take him up for the day in John's car. Around mid-morning I had a call from them to say that the brakes had failed but they had still managed to get to Keswick and take the car into a garage. However, they needed a part for it, so could I go to the dealer's to get it and bring it up. So I set off in the Fellowship's old Wolseley 1500, and after acquiring the part I arrived at lunch time at the pre-arranged car park. There was no sign of them but I found some chalk in the car so wrote on the ground that I had gone to get some chips and would be back soon. On my return, the Wolseley had disappeared and a new chalk message informed me 'Gone home' (the old car was very easy to break into!). It didn't take too long though to spot John and Fred hiding behind a car not far away with big smiles on their faces, while my car had been pushed away to another area. I think this typified the fact that although we were doing the serious job of running a church organisation, we also had a lot of fun and there was a real sense of love, commitment and unity between us.

One Monday night after a Whitsun conference, my friend

Clive from Birmingham rang me from Scotland. He was now staying with Jack Kelly, a top heart specialist who owned a big house in Lesmahagow, just south of Glasgow. Clive said he'd heard that we had Mr North with us and Jack was keen to meet him, and asked if I could bring him up on a visit.

Mr North was agreeable so next morning I drove him up in the old Wolseley 1500. The trip up was okay but rather quiet, as I was a bit over-awed at being with this revered speaker and pastor. I was still quite a quiet chap and really didn't know what to say to him. The scenery was nice though, which made it a pleasant trip. When we arrived, we found ourselves in a very grand house called Auchenheath house where Dr Kelly lived with his family and a few other folk, including my friend Clive. They were already having fellowship meetings in the house, and Jack had heard of Pastor North and wanted to hear what he was preaching.

I think it's fair to say they hit it off straight away and Mr North stayed on with them for some time, while I had to return to Liverpool the next day. That was to be the first of many trips to Auchenheath for me and many others over the years.

Later that year, I took my mum on holiday to South Wales for a week (not sure how I managed that!) and on another occasion she came up to Liverpool for a holiday to spend time with me. She liked coming and I would take her up to Crosby or over to West Kirby on the Wirral – like me she loved to go to the seaside. She also enjoyed helping in the kitchen in the fellowship house.

I also went down to Birmingham regularly to see her and make sure she was ok. On one occasion, I borrowed the house car, by that time a Ford Anglia which was more modern than the Wolesley but very basic compared with today's cars. I set out in the morning on a sunny day but while traveling down the M6 I thought the car was behaving badly so pulled over onto the hard shoulder and discovered a back tyre had gone flat. I went to the boot to get the spare wheel, only to find there were no tools or jack.

"Hmm," I thought, "now there's a problem," but then I looked at where I was and realised from traveling this road so often that there were Services about a mile or so further on, so I drove on up the hard shoulder very slowly to safety. When I got there I discovered my problems were not yet over; I had precisely two shillings and sixpence in my pocket (12½ pence in modern money)! However, not far from where I had parked was a breakdown van, so I went and explained my situation and lack of money and how I worked for the church. The man very kindly offered to come and change the wheel for me (maybe he was an angel in disguise!). I did offer him my 2/6 but he said he thought I needed it more than he did! I got to my destination and back safely that day thanking God.

In July, I was asked to go on a trip to Spain. Dick Hussey had got a house in the suburbs of Madrid and had asked if Peter Gray would come over with his tools and do a bit of carpentry for him. Roy Jones offered to drive him there in his Austin 1100 and I was asked to go as co-driver. "Great," I thought, "but when do I get time to do some decorating in the house?"

We had a good journey, uneventful apart from arriving at a French campsite late at night. It was dark and when we were setting up our ridge tent, the clatter we made woke up a load of moorhens in a nearby pond. They made so much noise that the whole campsite must have woken up with it. We didn't wait to find out in the morning, we got going quickly before anyone was around!

Camping in my old ridge tent on the way through France

We had a very pleasant two weeks in Spain. While Pete got down to work, Roy and I visited some of the tourist sites in Madrid and also spent some time with some old friends, Sandy and Pauline Frame, who were out there working for WEC, going for drinks with them in the street bars and swimming in a local lake.

Sandy Frame, Roy and Pete in Spain

On our return to Liverpool, I tried to settle into some sort of routine. I managed to wallpaper Fred's office, but unfortunately the paper he chose had a very distinctive pattern. After a while he noticed that people who came to see him were side-tracked into studying it and looking at the wall instead of listening to him, so I had to re- paper the room!

I did not have long to get on with jobs however, as John Val suggested that some of us should make a trip to Italy to visit Philip Wiles and the church where Daniela had come from. We arranged for John, me, Steve Davis and Lee Cheung to travel together and set off on Friday 1st September in John Val's works car. This was a nice Ford

Cortina and we managed to fit in all our gear, including my four-man ridge tent and also a large catering-size bag of cornflakes, which as the journey progressed gradually turned into a bag of corn crumbs, sufficing us nevertheless for our breakfasts throughout the journey.

Our journey progressed well down through France, but I realized that John wanted to go on a different route than the one I as Chief Map Reader had planned. He explained why: some years previously John had taken a group from the fellowship on a mission trip to Spain in an old ambulance; on the way back the engine had died leaving them stranded in a French village for several weeks until the RAC finally flew out a new part for the repair. The villagers had taken pity on them and kindly looked after them during the delay, so he just wanted to call in and visit them en route.

Arriving in the village, we stopped off at a farmhouse and the family were really pleased to see John and Steve and invited us all for dinner. We sat round an old wooden table in the kitchen. The room was not the cleanest I've ever seen, there was no paint on the walls and the sink was piled high with dirty pots and pans. The daughter pulled out 4 chicken legs from a drawer in the table, threw them into a frying pan with some garlic and fried them for a few minutes then they were served with some bread and wine. I have to say the meal was very tasty and we enjoyed it – and suffered no ill after-effects!

After this diversion from the direct route, we continued south. John then explained he just wanted to pop in and visit some folk in Spain while we were in the vicinity – it was probably only about a thousand miles diversion in the wrong direction, but he thought it wouldn't take long...

We arrived in Tamariu in northern Spain and spent a nice day there seeing John's friends and going to the sea front in the evening for drinks. We camped overnight, and after having our cornflakes/crumbs we continued on our journey east up through the French Riviera on a very fast motorway. John was driving at around 90 mph to try to catch up on some of the time we'd lost. It was a beautiful road with splendid views, full of tunnels and bridges. We were making good time and had crossed the border into Italy when suddenly the engine started spluttering, so John decided to pull over into a lay-by to check it. He found the brakes were not working very well either, and after trying them out a few times they were making some terrible grinding noises. There was nothing for it but to go on slowly and turn off at the next exit, leading gently downhill towards the resort of Allasio. At this point, the engine gave out completely and we coasted down into the town controlled only by the handbrake. We found, to our astonishment, a Ford dealership who offered to fix it overnight and recommended a reasonable hotel for us to stay in.

We had a very pleasant evening walking the promenade before getting an early night in what proved to be very comfortable beds. Next morning, we went back to the garage where to our relief the car was all fixed. The mechanic explained that the front brakes had completely worn out and the points in the distributer had broken, which he had never seen before in a car. We were thankful they had however, because if we had needed to brake at the 90 mph speed we'd been going at, it could have had serious accident.

Before resuming our journey, I rang Philip Wiles to say we were running a bit late in our schedule due to the breakdown and also to our 'slight' detour. He was relieved to hear from us, as he had been expecting us to arrive a few days before.

After the final 800 or so miles, we eventually arrived in Udine in north-east Italy, and had a nice time with Philip and his family. John preached in the church the next Sunday and we had good fellowship with the church members, then on the Monday Philip and Peggy and their daughter Sylvia took us on a day out over the nearby border into Yugoslavia! What an unexpectedly beautiful place that was, and such a lovely day we had.

The following week, we headed down the "leg" of Italy to Florence. We had been asked if we could visit a young man in prison there, who for some reason had been denied all visitors including the prison chaplain. Once more it was a high-speed journey down the motorways, arriving late in the afternoon. We went straight to the prison, but after an embarrassing half hour when our lack of Italian and the warders' lack of English made communication very difficult, we finally understood that we would be able to speak to the Governor the next morning.

We had been told to visit a place called 'Casa Cares' so we drove into the countryside near Florence to find it; it turned out to be an orphanage run by a Christian group of foreign nationals. Amazingly, there was a room here with four beds all made up as if they had been expecting us! We were given such a warm welcome by the people there.

After some food and meeting the staff and children, in the late evening we went into the nearby village where there was a fiesta going on. We had coffees in a street café and watched an amazing firework display.

Next morning, an American girl from the staff who spoke good Italian offered to come back with us to the prison to interpret. The prison Governor was ready for us on our return and we were able to ask about the young man and got permission to visit him. I don't remember much about the prisoner, but the main thing was that the Governor later promised to ensure the prison Chaplain could come to visit him regularly.

Mission accomplished, we left the American girl in the city centre as she had other business in Florence, and started on our journey of 230 miles back to Udine. I remember that at this point that I was worn out, hot (there was no air conditioning in cars in those days), tired of sitting navigating with a big map on my lap, and hungry because John just wanted to push on as much as he could. I know I was thinking to myself, I must remember not to come on a trip like this again. However, I must have forgotten all that because I did do it all again!

During our journey back to Udine, we stopped off in Venice for a quick look around (John got a ticket for parking in the wrong place!) before continuing the last leg and arriving at Philip's house in the early evening.

We spent another lovely day with Philip and Peggy before setting off on our return journey. Thankfully, we took a shorter route home (around 900 hundred miles), including one very frosty night camping on a mountain.

Needless to say, we had quite an interesting story to tell the church on our arrival back in Devy Road.

Thankfully, the rest of the 1971 was not quite so adventurous, but even so it included a couple of trips to Scotland, taking my mum on one of them for a few days' holiday, and a trip to Ripon with Fred.

My first year working in the house had turned out to be quite a year! Besides trips abroad I had returned to Birmingham quite often to see my mum and made other visits around the UK. It was always nice to get back to my new Liverpool home though and whenever I returned to the house, as I turned the final corner I would have a sense of excitement inside with all that God was doing and eager anticipation for what was going to happen next.

Chapter 3: Four just men

After Norman and Jenny left for the Longcroft and Dick and Sylvia Hussey went to Spain, we had four Elders leading the church. These men, all different, each brought something unique in their own way to the fellowship and were much loved.

Mr Moffat and his wife were in their early sixties. He was a retired teacher and their adult children Peter and Lorna were also in the fellowship, together with Lorna's husband Andy Hutchins. They were like a mum and dad to many, very caring and always there for you when you needed encouragement. Most folk in the church knew them affectionately as Mum and Dad Moffat.

In those early years of the fellowship, Mr Moffat organised and ran the annual Summer Conference, held at Cliff

College Bible School in Derbyshire. Around four to five hundred people from the various fellowships around the country gathered for a week to hear the preaching of Mr North and Norman Meeten. It must have been no small job for him in those days before home computers, as presumably all the work had to be done through the postal service.

Dave Wetherley was a carpenter who had worked full time in the fellowship since the Queens Rd days. When you met Dave you knew you had a friend for life; he was so loving and had the gift of making you feel you must be his best friend. When you were talking to him, you were the focus of his attention, nobody else. He would greet me with 'Jamie, dear brother, how are you?' and throw his big carpenter's arms around me. I would say I must surely have been a very special friend to him, but I think everyone felt that!

John Valentine, a single man, was the son of a docker. He was a big fellow with a big heart and a big voice. It was jokingly said of him that if he held an open air eeting down at the Pier Head, (traditionally the place where preachers went to speak in public in those days) he would also be heard over the water in Birkenhead. He had tremendous drive and energy which may account for him being so successful as a salesman. I think people viewed him as someone you could completely trust and rely on, which made him very appreciated in business circles as well as in church.

One time, my mum and I were on our way up to Auchenheath where together with John we were going to fit some kitchen units, and we called in at the factory where they made the chipboard John Val sold. John gave us a tour to show us how it was made. It was fascinating to see the huge machines turning it all out. After the production line tour, he showed us where they stored the finished chipboard, stacks and stacks of the stuff filling every part of the building. He pointed out to us that he had sold it all already, and they were having trouble keeping up with his orders.

The fourth elder, Fred Tomlinson, is shown here (on the right) with Mr Moffat. He lived with his wife Sheila and their three young children on the middle floor. They became a much-loved family and their door was always open for any who needed them or just wanted to pop in to have a chat. Quite often they would have many of the single young people in for the evenings when they were free.

When Fred had been in the police force he had passed the advanced driving test, pretty evident by his driving confidence. I travelled many times with him around the country, and saw how he overtook other cars with ease on busy roads, and often we reached our destination much quicker than if I'd been driving.

I can't remember much of Fred and John preaching in the meetings before they were made elders, but they both stepped up to their calling afterwards and quickly developed in their ministries and were much appreciated. In my opinion, it quite quickly became evident that Fred became the leading elder of the four.

The work of the house that Norman had established continued very much in the same vein. The meetings were for fellowship, worship and preaching of scripture and truth as had been taught by the New Testament church, and they continued to draw many from near and far. We also sang a lot of hymns written by Charles Wesley back in the 1700s.

John Wesley became a great preacher and it's said the history of Great Britain was changed through his ministry when he travelled the length and breadth of the country preaching in towns and villages and even in the open fields to crowds of thousands of people. John's brother Charles wrote many famous hymns which carried the religious revival forward for years to come. Looking back, I realize that many of these hymns strongly imbued our meetings with the same Holy Spirit through whom they were written.

As the fellowship churches grew, a group of people made a collection of 120 of these hymns and reprinted them in their original form, often including verses which had for whatever reason previously been omitted from modern hymn books. The new book was named 'Hymns of eternal truth' and sometimes jokingly referred to as 'Hymns of eternal length' – some of them run to 12 verses...

Back in those early days our Sundays consisted of a morning meeting at 10.30, a bit of lunch provided for any who wanted to stay (which was most people) and then an afternoon meeting at three pm. This one was started off by Norman Meeten so that any folk from other churches could come along too if they wanted to without neglecting their own church.

Also in those early days, as quite a few young people joined the fellowship, including many from universities, under Fred's leadership they began a smaller evening Sunday meeting down in the dining room, specifically to encourage us younger men into preaching and ministry. This influenced many young men who later went on into church leadership.

During the 1970s, no.14 Devonshire Rd remained open for people with various needs to come and stay; it was a place of healing in a loving safe haven for many.

One of these was a young man named Peter. He had been on drugs to some extent and they had affected his mind, putting him in quite a bad way. His sister had started bringing him along to the fellowship in the hope that he would be helped. He came with us all to one of the summer conferences at Cliff College and I was asked to look after him for the week. As I was also acting as driver taking some of the young people out on trips during the week, Peter ended up coming along too.

One day we took them on a visit to Sherwood Forest; we went exploring and discovered what was supposed to be Robin Hood's cave. While the teenagers were enjoying looking inside it, Peter decided to sit down outside. This was not a good idea as it was on the edge of a cliff and after a short while he started leaning over backwards towards the cliff edge. We hastily managed to catch hold of him, thankfully before he went over!

Next day I took them all to a local outdoor swimming pool and again Peter had to come with us. He joined the others in the pool and was swimming lengths happily for a while then suddenly he just stopped and began to sink to the bottom. I was watching at the side of the pool, having been given a whistle to use as necessary to control bad behaviour. I didn't know what to do about Peter so decided to give a loud toot on the whistle, bringing the whole swimming pool to immediate complete silence with all eyes on me (very embarrassing!). I shouted to get some of our folk to rescue Peter from the bottom; they got him out and thankfully he was ok. At this point, I must admit I didn't hold out much hope for him and felt he was beyond help.

That evening however, Pastor North preached a powerful sermon in the meeting and as he concluded, he said to the congregation that if they wanted God to do something new in their lives they should cry out to Jesus. As we bowed in prayer, there was a sudden loud cry from the back of the hall and Peter ran to the front where he received prayer. The following morning as I walked down the hill from the dormitories to get my breakfast, what did I see but Peter sitting outside having a haircut looking a completely different person. I was astonished!

From that time on Peter was a changed young man. He got a job later in an electrical wholesaler's where one of the men from church worked and became a valued, loved member of the fellowship as well as a good friend and workmate to me in later years – but that's another story.

I want to be completely honest and add that we were not successful with everybody who came to the fellowship for help in those days. One young man was sent to us by his parents in desperation. X had serious mental health problems and had decided he no longer needed his medication. As a result, he was acting very strangely. (In those days we had little understanding of mental health issues, which didn't help.)

The first evening after dark X climbed onto the garage roof at the back of the house and began howling like a dog. There was no one else around so I had to deal with the situation. I asked him to come down – unsuccessfully – then, because it was very dark out there, I went inside the house putting lights on in every room, which you could say brought light on the situation, and thankfully he decided to come down. He ended up having to sleep in my bedroom that night in Brett's bed, which was rather scary especially when I woke up to see him getting out of bed and coming towards me. "Uh oh," I thought, "I've had it now!" but thankfully he just wanted to open the window a little bit, phew!

Next evening, things deteriorated further and X was becoming violent. Fred, John and Dave Wetherley felt there was nothing more we could do and we'd have to take him home to his parents so they could get medical help for him. We had to manhandle him to get him into John's car and restrain him during the journey home. It became quite confusing in the dark with the wrong hands being squeezed at times – bringing a little amusement among us – but overall it was a terribly sad situation where we couldn't help X.

There is one more person I feel to mention here. Alison was in a psychiatric ward in a local hospital when we heard of her. Dad Moffat was involved in getting her transferred to come and live at the house. She had self-harmed in the past and had had a leucotomy/lobotomy performed on her, which I suspect had made her condition worse. (These operations are no longer performed). Despite her difficulties she was accepted as part of the fellowship family and lived next door in the girls' flat. She needed a lot of loving and patience from us all as she was a very troubled person.

Although there was no great instant miracle in her life, Alison slowly started to improve but still had the occasional slip up. One evening after she'd had an upset, she announced to me that she was going to go and talk to Lesley Cobill. The only trouble was that Lesley was now living in a fellowship North Wales. Alison immediately set off to walk there and as there was no one around to ask for help, there was nothing for it but for me to accompany her on her journey (in my bedroom slippers).

Thankfully after walking nearly a mile towards the Mersey Tunnel Alison started to feel tired and we sat on a wall just below the Anglican Cathedral. As we sat there chatting, I was wondering what to do. I couldn't leave her to go and find a phone box and she would never make it walking back to the house as it was mostly uphill. As I was pondering over my situation, Dad Moffat drove past in his green VW Beetle. He must have just caught a glimpse of us sitting there. He gave a little wave and drove on a short distance before stopping and reversing to see why we were sitting on a wall so far from the house with me still in my slippers.

As we drove back home I gave an account of what had happened and Mr Moffat spent some time that evening with Alison, counselling and praying with her, which I believe was of much help to her. He told me afterwards that he very rarely drove over to the fellowship in the evenings other than for meetings, but on this particular night he felt constrained to come and attend to some minor business. It's amazing how God works in these situations, even down to directing him on the route he chose to come so that it brought him past us sitting on a wall. Thank God!

Alison continued to improve and eventually managed to get a flat in a sheltered housing complex where she managed to look after herself. After I left Liverpool later on, Pete and Sue Moffatt and others continued to lovingly look out for her and she was a blessing to many.

Alison passed away some years ago now and went to be with the Lord she loved. It was testimony to her life that among those who came to celebrate her life at her funeral was one of the doctors from the local health centre she attended. Alison may not have had an instant miracle but over the years she steadily improved, which was still very wonderful considering all she had gone through and the medical view of her when we were first introduced all those years ago.

Chapter 4: Further trips to Italy 1972

Daniela, her mother Pierina, and now baby Sara had been with us in Liverpool for almost a year (see Chapter 2). When we discovered they only had passports for a year, we had to start working out how to get them back home to Italy. However, before that journey could take place, just before Christmas 1971 John Val took them along with others from the fellowship on a short holiday to Kelso in Scotland. My wife-to-be, Jean, who at that point had been coming to the fellowship for only a few months, says that the night before the trip, John asked if she would like to come along too and then went to see her father to promise he would look after her and also pay for it all. She says they all had a great time and a lot of fun. John, true to form, had them all going round the care homes and pubs in the area carol singing and giving their testimonies!

For me, the year ended quietly. I went home to spend Christmas with Mum, Grace and John, then I was back in Devy Road for the new year conference.

We then began to plan how to get Daniela and Pierina back home. During their stay they had acquired quite a few more belongings than those they had come with, so trains or planes were out of the question.

Mr Moffat borrowed a Land Rover from one of his friends, Jack Frost, who lived down in Kings Langley. The Moffats then started organising the trip and asked me to go along to help, along with Julia Hardy who would interpret for us all. We set off on 8th February, and I think my outstanding memory of the whole journey is how cold it was. The heater in the Land Rover was not very effective, so we kept our coats on all the time; I only had some rather thin leather boots and socks, so my feet were really cold.e on French soil, we headed south. We didn't go on any motorways in France which made the journey quite interesting, passing through the countryside and many small villages. At lunchtimes, it became evident why our Land Rover was fully loaded: Mr and Mrs Moffat had brought everything bar the kitchen sink! Every lunchtime out came a gas cooker and a meal was cooked.he journey took a few days and with Julia's language help we found a hotel or guest house each night. Once we were settled in, I had to smuggle food and a small gas stove up to my room to make tea or supper. The downside of that was Mr Moffat coming in very early each morning while I was still asleep, to brew up tea for himself and Mrs Moffat!

Finally, after a year of being away, Pierina, Daniela and baby Sara arrived home in Udine. We spent a week with them, getting them settled in and taking them round to visit various family members. This included a visit up to Sauris Di Sotto, way up in the mountains, where they had rooms in the large family house. An uncle there had a family business in curing hams which over the years has grown to be very large and well known in Italy.

Sauris di Sotto from Daniela's window in winter.................

The lake below the village

The journey to get there was an adventure in itself, going up steep twisting roads, through tunnels and over bridges, and made all the more exciting as there was at least two feet of snow on the ground as we climbed higher to the village.

We were given a warm welcome by the family and stayed the night in the big house. When I finally got to bed that cold night, I found what looked like a large copper frying pan with a lid on in my bed. On inspection, I saw it contained hot embers from the fire, and it made my bed lovely and warm to get into – just like an old English warming pan.

While we were in Italy, we made a little foray into Yugoslavia, as Mr Moffat wanted to go there. As we travelled along towards Trieste, he suddenly announced that he remembered driving just there during the war in an armoured scout car, when they came under fire from the Germans and had to turn back quickly, fortunately without any harm done.

After we had stayed in Udine for seven days Mr Moffat felt it was time for our departure. We had been staying with various church members and we didn't want outstay our welcome there. It was sad to leave Pierina, Daniela and Sara; I'm not sure how easy it was for them to return to the church. We loved them and I felt it was not the end of the story as far as I was concerned.

After leaving, we travelled down south, calling into Venice for a few hours (it was cold and damp) then on to Padova, then to Florence where Mr Moffat showed us round the cathedral which he seemed to know a lot about. Then we went on to Casa Cares, which I had previously visited with John Val as he was keen also to visit it.

Once more, the folk there were very welcoming and offered us food and accommodation for the night. I think this was the worst night of the trip for me; I shared a room with another chap and it was so cold I spent the night trying in vain to get my feet warm. In the morning before departing, Mr Moffat enjoyed speaking with the children, doing little stories and I think tricks to amuse them.

On our way back up through France, on the Sunday we stopped off at a small church we had noticed on our outward journey. I think their morning service had just finished and people welcomed us, and the pastor invited us to lunch. I can distinctly remember the drink which we had with the meal; it was like a peppermint cordial which I had never had before and I wasn't sure if it was a mouth wash or something! I managed to drink it though. Julia tells me that that visit began a link which she continues to have to this day. Finally, we arrived back in England on 29th February after being away for three weeks.

While we were in Italy, I noticed that nearly everyone had electric door locks in their homes to let visitors in. I was very impressed and thought this would be an ideal solution to the house situation where we were constantly having to run upstairs to answer the doorbell.

I managed to buy one at a very reasonable price and on return fitted it to the front door connecting it to a button in the kitchen. The result was very satisfying, particularly at tea times, when the bell rang, instead of people reluctantly having to run up to answer it, they were all racing to see who could press the button first.

It did need tweaking a bit, I had to fit an intercom system so we knew who was at the door after an incident involving the postman who came one day with a parcel and after ringing the bell, there was a click and the door opened but there was no one there which left him very confused.

The system served us well for many years but is no longer in use now although the lock is still there and still working fine after 50 years.

Later in the year, John Val suggested a return trip to Italy to see how Pierina and Daniela were going on. I was keen to go and in fact this time there were more folk wanting to come with us, so we travelled in two cars. In our car the group was the same as last time and in the second car, driven by Christopher Powis, were Julia Hardy, Louise Wilson and Katy Lee. Here are Steve, me, Louise and Katy.

I wasn't surprised when we took the same route down through France to Spain, the only difference being that we didn't have any breakdowns. One nice thing that did happen though was with Chris. He was a gardener (horticulturist) and was taking great interest in the plant life and nature as we travelled south through France. However, when we got to Tamariu in Spain, his focus was turning more onto Julia and a blossoming romance began.

(They married in August the following year)

Our time in Udine was short but we went up to Sauris where Pierina and Daniela were staying. It was so lovely to see them again and to discover little Sara was growing up so fast.

Julia with Sara and Daniela

Our return journey went ok except that while we were in the mountains, John happened to hit a large rock on the side of a narrow road; this put the front wheel alignment out a little which resulted in the tyre making a screeching noise all the way home!

I thought that would be enough travels for that year, but a couple in the fellowship (Morris and Sarah Bowness) had move to Germany and they asked if I could bring some of their belongings out to them in my van. Roy Jones agreed to come along, and I also asked Lesley Cobill if she would come, as I had heard that Sarah had no female company out there and I thought it would be good for her.

Germany proved to be a beautiful country. The highlight of that trip, besides seeing Morris and Sarah and the lovely scenery, was a tour round the famous Leica camera factory which Morris worked for in Sales. It was interesting to see all the men working at benches putting these famous cameras together. Needless to say, we weren't given any freebies as the cameras sold for around a thousand pounds back then. As consolation, Roy and I had our photos taken by Morris on a Leica camera.

After a pleasant week in Wetzlar, Germany, we arrived back in Liverpool safely in time for Christmas and I went home to spend time with Mum, John and Grace again. It was strange knowing that Birmingham was no longer my home and I looked forward to getting back to Liverpool.

The new year conference started in Liverpool the following weekend, and there was much to be done in preparing for it, with accommodation to be sorted out for the many people who were coming from all over the country. It was a busy time for all those working in the house and afterwards there was the big clear up. Thankfully, the following day I had my day off and went to the Longcroft for some peace and quiet and a well-earned rest.

During those years, many deep bonds of friendship were

formed. Most of us were in our 20s with not a lot of money, and most lived in flats in the Toxteth area near Devy Road. There was a real sense of looking out for one another and helping out when there were needs – my van became very handy for this. I was often invited for a meal in the evenings by families or those living together in flats, so I got to know quite a few people really well. I could mention so many by name – but where do you start?! 50 years on, most of them are scattered around the country and even around the world, but thanks to email, Facebook and other media we remain in touch with many. (I see I have 250 friends on Facebook!)

In the four years I lived and worked at the house, besides the work that went on there and the meetings which we had been so blessed in, we also had lots of fun together as friends. This included a few days out on coach trips, one which Fred and I organized to Conwy. We went out there together in Fred's car a week previously to check it out and get ideas of what was there. We took a walk up to the castle to get the admission prices and when they found we were bringing a coach party they told us to go in for free and have a look round. It found it very interesting but on the day of the trip we felt a bit bad because we all just went up to the up to the Sychnant Pass, some walking there over the hills from Conwy and the rest of us by coach for a picnic and games.

John Valentine organized another trip to Keswick which was a lot of fun too. A lot of us went on a pleasure boat trip round the lake and while boarding it we nearly dropped Danny Singleton over the side while trying him to carry him onto the boat in his wheelchair.

A lot of our folk sat in the back of the boat and sang Christian songs all the way round. I was a bit worried that some of the other passengers might be offended but when we got off many of them thanked us and said we had kept them entertained.

During this period too there were many relationships formed which started off a spate of weddings. On most of these occasions, to keep the cost down the ladies in the church would organize the catering for the reception, and we fellows would do all the grafting to prepare the meeting place and act as ushers. In my third year of working in the house, that summer we had five weddings on successive weekends – lovely but also a bit exhausting for us all!

With all that was going on during this time, I was beginning to wonder if marriage would ever happen to me. Although I was living in the centre of all this activity, I sometimes felt a bit lonely. There was a hymn we used to sing, *Thine be the glory, risen conquering son*, which had a line in it which went, 'Aid us in our strife.' I changed this to sing 'Aid us get a wife!' This prayer was soon to be answered!

I did have a best friend though, Brett, fellow Brummy and room-mate. You could say he was a bit of a character. He was very thin in those days – it was said he could hide behind a broom handle. He worked for ICI in Runcorn and went there each day riding a huge old motor bike, which you wondered how he managed because it must have been so heavy. This is a picture of him when he used to run the Sunday-school.

In the Devy Road house at that time, the water was heated by an old coke boiler which I often had to look after, but others also fed it from time to time, including Brett. It was somewhat temperamental though and could overheat very easily if not adjusted properly. Often, Brett would set it to heat up quickly but then forget to go back to change it to normal heat. The result would be just steam coming out of the taps and then brown water. (To be fair, maybe sometimes it would be brown water when I did it too.)

Later when Brett married Maretta, I was his Best Man and he was mine when I eventually got married.

Chapter 5:

A significant year – 1973

My third year in the house, 1973, turned out to be a significant one for me. I was still going down to Birmingham regularly to see Mum and make sure she was all right. In June I took her to Aberystwyth for a week's holiday in Gerald James' hotel on the sea front. Gerald was very kind to us and took us out to several places of interest during our stay. He was holding Christian meetings in the hotel that week which he invited residents to attend, and he asked me to speak at one of them. Mum and I both loved the seaside and we had such a lovely holiday together.

Grace and I were becoming concerned about Mum at this point. John and Grace had had a baby and were wanting to move to a bigger house, which would mean she would be living in the cottage by herself. We knew she loved coming up to Liverpool so we decided that she should move up to be with me, which she was very happy to do.

She came in mid-August and had her own room in the fellowship house on the ground floor, and was soon enjoying helping out in the kitchen. I think it must have been a big move for her leaving her home and all her family in Birmingham, but she seemed to settle well and made lots of friends in the church and was happy there.

It was nice for me too and I often took her out for the day when I had time off. There are still other folk around now who tell me she was a lovely person and great to have in the house at that time. Here is Mum having a nap in the dining room after working in the kitchen.

By this time my travel adventures seemed to have become a regular part of life working in the fellowship house. In July, I made another trip with Roy Jones to Germany to visit Morris and Sarah again for a week. They took us out for picnics and swimming at local open-air pools as it was very hot. My outstanding memories are: 1) The German frankfurters with mustard were amazing and 2) Germans don't know how to queue up to buy food at a kiosk!

Roy and I with Sarah, in Wetslar.

I should point out here that there were others in the church who had travel adventures at this time – some were going on mission trips. Around this time a man known as Brother Andrew had written a book called 'Open Doors' describing how he had been led to start smuggling Bibles to Christians behind the Iron Curtain and to bring help to those who were being persecuted for their faith. As a result of this Phil Williamson and others of our folk started to make visits to churches in Russia to bring encouragement and Bibles to them. They brought back some interesting and exciting stories to tell the church.

There were also some groups going out to Sweden to visit and help Andy and Lorna Hutchins, who were now living in a large house on the banks of the Baltic Sea and were having meetings in the house for many local Swedish folk.

Andy and Lorna asked if I could also make a trip out in my caravanette to take some of their belongings that they had left behind when they moved out there. So, in October, along with Mr and Mrs Moffat and Sue Withey, we set off with my van fully loaded and a settee strapped to the roof. (In order to make enough space I'd had to strip all the cupboards and seats out!) We set off over the Pennines to Hull to catch the ferry. Peter Moffat brought Sue over in his car to make that part of the journey more comfortable for the rest of us. (I think Pete and Sue were not quite going out together at this point.)

It was rather windy going up to Hull, and when we reached the ferry the cover we had put over the settee was in shreds. I guess this should have given us some warning of what was about to come when we got out to sea. Once beyond the harbour, the full force of the gale hit us. Initially it was quite exciting, but we soon headed for our bunks for the night, finding it was a bit more comfortable to lie down, and we tried to shut our ears to the people around us being seasick.

Thankfully we woke to a quiet morning and enjoyed the rest of the journey, particularly when we sailed through the islands at sunset on the approach to our destination, Gothenburg.

We had a very enjoyable four weeks there, being invited out for meals by friends in the fellowship, rowing round the many islands, fishing (caught nothing) and a trip across the Baltic to visit Allan and Maija Scotson in Helsinki for a few days.

It was particularly nice for Mr and Mrs Moffat to have time with their daughter Lorna and son-in-law Andy.

At the end of the month, we travelled uneventfully back home with an empty van.

On my return it was back into the routine of my work and I was pleased to find my mum was still enjoying being at the house and helping in the kitchen.

Shortly after my return, I had to go one evening to visit May

Jackson, affectionately known by everyone in the fellowship as Auntie May. I must have only stayed a short while as I had another person to see afterwards. As she walked me to the gate, I asked if she knew where the road was that I needed to visit next, or if she had an A-Z map (no satnavs back then). Unfortunately, she didn't, but just at that point Jean Thorpe came up to see her. Jean was Auntie May's real niece and lived with her mum and dad about a hundred metres down the road. She'd been coming to the fellowship for quite a while by then, so I knew her a bit. She offered to run home to get a map for me and as she went, something about her seemed to catch my eye and attract my attention. "Hmm," I thought, "she's rather nice!"

The following week I was going to visit Mr and Mrs Moffat for the evening, and I asked Jean if she would like to come with me. I'm not sure what they thought when we arrived together on the doorstep! Anyway, I felt we got on quite naturally together during the evening, and when I dropped her home again in my caravanette, I gave her a box of chocolates and felt like kissing her!. So that was the beginning of our relationship which grew and blossomed quickly into romance.

It was nice that my mum was here in Liverpool at that time; I was 27 years old that November and she saw me start courting Jean and said she really liked her. Not long after this, Mum had a real disappointment. She had lived in the fellowship house since arriving in the summer, but after I got back from Sweden the room was needed for other things, so she had to move. She managed to get a bedsit only a few hundred yards away in Princes Avenue and moved in, I think it was at the beginning of December. I seem to recall she was starting to feel tired quite a lot of the time, but she continued coming to all the meetings and enjoyed them. I visited her every day if I could and often had lunch with her.

We had a Christmas party in late December and during it we all sang a song that someone had brought back from Nigeria. It went "Will you be ready when the Lord shall come?", and then the second part was "Oh yes, I will be ready, I will be ready when the Lord shall come." Mum was on her feet and seemed to really enjoy singing this song.

The following weekend was the New Year conference which we all enjoyed. Mum was in all the meetings and seemed fine, but on Monday morning she was missing. Jean felt anxious about this and said we should go straight round to see her when the meeting ended. The curtains were still closed when we got there and there was no reply when we rang the bell. We rang the landlady's bell, but she said she hadn't seen Mum. We noticed that there was a window in Mum's flat that was slightly open, so the landlady got a young man who was a resident there to climb in and open the door for us. To our great dismay and shock, there was Mum lying on the floor. It looked as though she'd had a fall in the night, and we quickly discovered she couldn't speak or move, which made it pretty evident that she'd had a stroke. We put a cover over her while the landlady went to ring for an ambulance, and Jean suggested I should pray for her, which I did although with difficulty through my tears.

We both went with her in the ambulance and saw her admitted to the Southern Hospital. Next day when I went to visit she was sitting up in bed and looking better, but still unable to talk or move her right arm. The amazing thing was that she was cheerful and pleased to see me, although a little frustrated that she couldn't communicate. Jean told me that normally people who have had a stroke sink into depression and frustration from not being able to talk, but in all the time Mum was in hospital she remained her usual happy self. When she tried to tell us things and couldn't get the word out, she would even laugh at herself!

During January, I went in nearly every day to visit her. The nurses were wonderful and let me come and go as I pleased – one of them asked me one day if I had a season ticket because I'd come so often! Jean also called in the evenings and on her days off work. She did Mum's hair for her as she'd been a hairdresser before she started nursing. John and Grace also came up from Birmingham each week. On one occasion, when Grace took young Lorna to the hospital with her, Mum was so delighted to see her she actually said, "Hello Lorna!" That was the one and only time Mum ever said anything again.

After about three weeks one of the staff told me that if Mum did recover, it was going to be a long slow process, and that we should try to find a place for her as they would need the bed for others. I was feeling quite tired by now and suggested to Jean that we take a short break to give time to consider what I was going to do in these circumstances. So we went up to Scotland in the last week of January to stay at Auchenheath House. While we were away, John and Grace came up to Liverpool and visited Mum every day.

We had a pleasant few days up there, going out to my birthplace and Loch Lomond, and we also took the opportunity to call on some of my uncles and aunts and introduce Jean to them. During this time of course it was uppermost in our minds what to do about Mum. Jean suggested that we could get married, get somewhere to live, and look after her together, which I thought was very lovely of her.

On the Thursday, we went out for the day. We found a nice view of the Forth Bridge and sat there for a while discussing the options and praying for guidance. On our return to Auchenheath in late afternoon, Dave Weatherly (who was also staying there doing some work) was waiting on the doorstep and greeted us with the news that Mum had passed away earlier that day; she'd had a massive heart attack. Marion, one of the ladies who worked there, came and gave me a big hug as the tears flowed; we were both shocked by the news.

We decided to go home later that day. Dave said he would come along with us too, so we sorrowfully packed up and after the evening meal set off for Liverpool. We were in Jean's car, a Triumph Herald which wasn't very fast, so we didn't get back till the early hours of the morning. John and Grace met us on our return, as they had stayed up to let us in.

Next day, before they returned to Birmingham, John kindly went to the undertakers to make the necessary arrangements for the funeral. Mum passed away on 31st January 1974, she would have been 68 on 9th February.

The funeral was held on 6th February, and quite a few of our relatives from Birmingham came up for it. The service was held in the meeting room in the fellowship house led by Fred, and Norman Meeten led the committal at the graveside. Although it was such a sad occasion, the message of hope and assurance of eternal life came through powerfully.

I don't mind admitting, though, I was sad and shed a few tears – I don't think grief is wrong! Mum had always been part of our lives, always there to encourage and quietly help through times of difficulty in our life journey. She had worked hard to bring up Grace and me when we were young and had managed to take us on holidays every year, often to Butlins for a week or even two weeks, where we'd had such great fun, boating, swimming, horse riding and more.

I spoke to Sandra Hitchiner, who was working in Devy Rd at that time. She told me my mum was a very humble, simple straightforward lady, who was a blessing to everyone she spoke to, and that I should be proud that she'd been my mum. I also had quite a few letters from different folk afterwards telling me how much she'd been loved and appreciated. One came from a pastor, known affectionately by all as Uncle Tom. He was in Australia when he heard the news, and commented that Mum had often written to him and said how proud she was of Grace and me, and she told him about all we were doing and what we were involved with.

Another lady, Margaret Jardine Smith, who had assisted in the house for a short time, wrote to say what a help Mum had been to them when they had to cater for so many, and her presence had helped keep them calm; she'd been a real blessing.

After the funeral, we had some refreshments back at the house. My Uncle Jack (who was known for giving little speeches) got up and said that the family had been concerned about Mum moving so far away from them to come to Liverpool, but he could see she had many lovely friends here which they were thankful for, and now they could understand why she did it.

Over the next few days, I received several gifts of money from people. I thought this was very kind, and when shortly afterwards I got a bill from the undertakers for £106, I knew why I'd got the money! Obviously I was able to pay the bill, and I still have the receipt!

I was so thankful to God that He had brought Jean into my life at this point; she was such a comfort, blessing and strength to me. I think all that happened helped our relationship grow more quickly.

In the Bible, St Paul wrote these words:

> 'And we know that in all things God works for the good of those who love him, who have been called according to his purpose.

A few weeks after this I caught the flu, and Auntie May kindly had me to stay for a few days to get over it. While I was there, of course Jean came to see me. One night, we sat in the front lounge chatting for a while, then I got down on one knee and asked if she would marry me. Over the years since, she has jokingly said she wonders if I was delirious with the flu at the time! "Ah," I reply, "but did you know what you were letting yourself in for when you said yes?" We decided we would marry in January 1975. To this day we still don't know why we chose January! At the time of writing this, we have been married for 45 years so I can't have been all that bad! Jean has been a wonderful wife and mother of three, as future episodes of my life story will reveal.

Chapter 6: Jean Thorpe

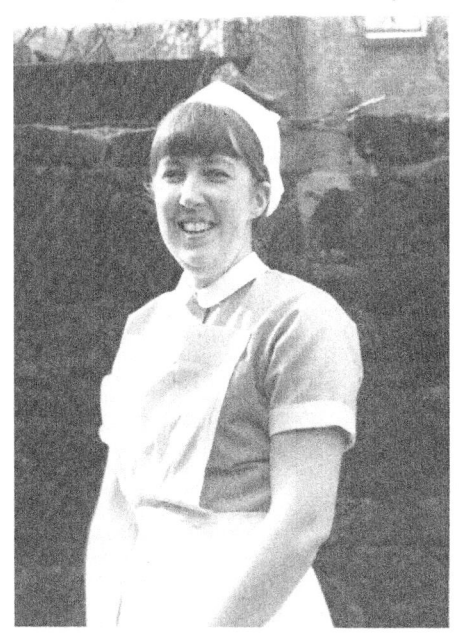

Jean's parents, David and Florence Thorpe, married in 1936 at Laurel Road Methodist church and moved into a newly built house in Childwall which they rented initially until a time came when they were able to get a mortgage like many others on the new estate. They were members of Cottenham Baptist church in Kensington. The church had originally been founded by four godly men who bought four terraced houses in Cottenham Street and removed the insides from them all, converting the building into a church building. A great many people started attending and a move of God was experienced where many had true conversion experiences.

Mr and Mrs Thorpe became valued members of the church and very involved there. Dave was the treasurer and taught in the Sunday school and Boys Brigade, while Florence played the piano for the services.

Dave worked for a heating and ventilating firm in Liverpool. He was a manager, and drew up the plans for the various jobs that came their way. One of these was to prepare the plans for heating a convent, for which he had to get special permission from the Pope to enter the building. During the second world war he was sent to work in Scotland. He had to sign the Official Secrets Act to work there and he never told anyone what he did. He was well respected and loved by everyone in the firm, even down to the cleaners who loved him lots.

Florence, Jean's mum, known as Flo to her husband and friends, worked in Blackler's, one of those old-fashioned stores in Liverpool which sadly no longer exist. She worked in sales along with her sister, and I can tell from some of the stories relayed to me that they had lots of fun and amusing happenings there.

When they married she gave up work to be a mother and housewife which was more the norm in those days. They had three children, John, Dorothy (better known as Dot) and finally Jean. Jean grew up in much the same way as I did, with lots of friends in the road where they lived. She played out with them constantly, often till late at night, and they frequently went off for the day with butties and a drink, over the fields (now all built on) without any cares or worries. Jean's dad was the only one in the road who had a car (and that was a works one). Jean left school at fifteen with no qualifications, although she did well in class, coming fourth overall.

Jean's dad was a keen fan of Liverpool football club and she often went to home games with him, standing in the Paddock and Anfield Rd end. She is still a loyal supporter and likes to watch all the games, but only on the television now. She tells me that often on Sundays on their return from church, he would see one of his neighbours doing his garden and stop to discuss with him the finer points of a recent game and the rest of the family would have to get out of the car and walk the rest of the way!

After leaving school, Jean did a three-year apprenticeship in hairdressing and then got a job in a shop where she made some lovely friends among those who worked there. After a while she left there and bought an Austin A35 van and started her own mobile hairdressing business. It was during this period that she went through a bit of a dark patch and suffered a spell of depression, so she was signed off work by her doctor.

I first met Jean during her time off work. Her sister Dot and her Auntie May had started coming to church and they asked Norman Meeten if he would visit Jean.

As a result of these visits, on Norman's recommendation, she went to stay with Norman and Jenny at the Longcroft for two months with the doctor's agreement; he was very supportive considering he was Jewish. He was amazed and pleased at her progress on her return visit.

As a result, she started coming to the fellowship and began her road to recovery. She made many friends in the church, in particular Ruth and Ann (who were two of her bridesmaids when we married four years later). I think I first noticed her during this time because the three of them always seemed to be having great fun together and were always laughing.

During that period after she had joined the fellowship, Jean went on a coach trip to Chester with the ladies from Page Moss Lane Baptist Church. While she was there she saw a display advertising for people take up a career in nursing; after talking to the nurses doing the display she felt drawn to it and took the leaflets. After prayer she felt the Lord was leading her into nursing. Later on, she applied and was accepted to go on the training course to become a State Enrolled Nurse.

From how she describes her time in nursing to me now, I get the impression she became a very good nurse and worked her way through the different departments in what was then Sefton General hospital (it was on the site where the Sefton Asda is now). She moved through surgical wards, operating theatres, then on to Alder Hay children's hospital for three months' training in caring for babies and children, and then three months' training in geriatrics in Princes Park hospital in Upper Parliament St.

She finished her training in Mosley Hill hospital which was then linked with Sefton General in those days. After she finished her training and became an SEN she stayed on there and made many friends. I gather she was a natural in her job, loved by patients and staff alike.

There was of course a lot of studying involved before she could become an SEN, but in the fellowship back then we had Ron Baker and Val Wigley (later married) who were both nursing tutors in Broad Green Hospital and kindly gave her a helping hand in preparing for the exams, which she passed first time. Several friends in the fellowship took her out for a Chinese meal to celebrate her success, but I didn't know her very well then so I missed out on that one!

After we had married, Jean left her nursing career to work in the fellowship, but her time there was short lived because she soon became pregnant with our daughter Jennifer, who was born on 4th November 1975 and has been such a blessing to us.

Although Jean left nursing, her caring abilities certainly came in handy in later life, as did her skills in hairdressing.

Chapter 7: 1974: My final trip to Italy

During this year I had continued to correspond with Philip Wiles in Italy, and he suggested I make another visit to the church in Udine. Steve Davis said he'd like to come too, so we planned to make a trip in August and I proceeded to let Philip know of our plans. However, as the time drew closer, Steve found he wouldn't be able to come with me after all. Having committed myself to going, I felt I'd have to proceed by myself. I had done quite a lot of trips abroad by this then, but this was the first time to go on my own, so while I was excited about it there was also a tinge of apprehension. There seemed to be no alternative, though, so I just got on with planning it.

I thought the best way to get there would be to fly and was recommended to speak to Mike Coles. Mike had a travel bureau in Exeter used by many people who were going on missions. He was able to get me a flight from Heathrow to Milan for £40 return; that sounds cheap now, but back then it was probably two weeks' wages for me had I still been in a paid job.

As previously mentioned, the principle for those living and working in the fellowship house was that we trusted God to provide for all our needs. As the time approached for me to pay for my tickets, I only had £30. On hearing this, Fred decided to give me £10 from church funds to make up the difference. However, I did wonder why that had happened, as I believed that God knew all my needs, so my faith was tested somewhat. It was only on my return home that I found a letter from Philip Wiles containing £10 waiting for me – it came after my departure! (The post to and from Italy can be very slow, even today!) I think God allows these things to happen both to test our faith and also to deepen our faith and trust in Him. There was another effect of the delayed post, which will become evident as the story proceeds.

Keith and Christine Kelly got married on 20th July, and I filmed it on my 8mm cine camera. Then on Monday 22nd, Jean took me down to Lime St station for an early morning train to London. I was surprised to find some of the church people had come to see me off, and at the last moment Fred showed up too. He said he'd suddenly realized the time and jumped in his car, and it felt like the very next minute he was at the station. After fond farewells, I was on my way.

Arriving at Heathrow in the early afternoon, I got through ticket and passport control easily and boarded the plane. I felt a mixture of excitement and trepidation as this was my first time flying, but soon we were in the air and I settled back to enjoy the journey. Not long into the flight, the stewardesses brought round a lovely pork steak meal; unfortunately, I didn't know this was part of the flight costs and had just had a sandwich in the airport – but I managed to eat it, just the same.

I was sitting next to two young businessmen who were quite interested to hear why I was going to Italy and especially that this was my first time flying. They suggested I tell the stewardess it was my maiden flight, as she would take me through to meet the captain and have a look round the cockpit. Much to my regret, I didn't follow their advice as I was too shy, but they compensated me later by swapping seats to let me sit next to the window. I had a magnificent view as we flew over the snow-covered mountains before coming into Italy and landing in Milan.

Once through customs, I discovered that my hoped-for lift with Philip across to Udine had not transpired; this was because my letter to him had not arrived in time. I tried phoning him at his apartment in Vercelli but there was no answer, so eventually I realized that I had to make my own way to Udine, a journey of around 250 miles. I figured it would have to be by train.

Eventually, by early evening I arrived at the Milan station ticket office and made efforts to request a ticket to Udine. The man behind the counter seemed rather reluctant to sell me a ticket though, and kept going on about the *carrozza*. I was totally confused but eventually an elderly gentleman waiting behind me stepped forward and spoke with the man who then was willing to sell me a ticket. This same gentleman took me along to the correct platform and waited with me for the train, which came as it grew dark. (The mosquitoes were out in force by this time and had a good meal on my ankles.) It turned out that my

Good Samaritan was going to the same destination, and eventually he helped me to understand that only the first three carriages (*carrozza*) were going to our destination, the others were splitting off for somewhere else. He not only got me on the right train but also managed to find us seats, where I soon dozed off for the entire journey, finally reaching Udine at around7.00 a m the following day.

After making my way to the church, I was greeted by Rosario, the young pastor, who showed me where I would be sleeping in the church flat. Then I made my way over to Philip and Peggy's where we spent a pleasant morning chatting, drinking lovely Italian coffee sitting on their balcony which looked out to the mountains in the distance. It had been an epic and memorable journey!

The next four weeks were taken up with work on the church, which needed decorating. Philip's son Peter was also there for the summer, and we soon became good friends and worked together a lot, both in church and in visiting people in the area, amongst many other things. I also spent time visiting Daniela and Pierina and young Sara in their flat in the town. It was lovely to see them again and I went to visit quite often when I could to have a chat and also to do some decorating for them.

One thing I loved during my stay was the walk from the church in Via Antonio Caccia down to Daniela's flat in the town centre. It took about ten minutes going down tree-lined streets past gated apartments, through a lovely park into the town to her road, Via Treppo.

During my four weeks I also had a few days out, together with Philip and Peggy, Peter and their daughter Sylvia; this picture was taken on a day trip to the beach.

I went with Rosario, Peter and another lad to Venice for a day, then we spent the night sleeping under the stars by the beach.

The highlight of my time there was when Daniela took Peter and me up to her family home in Sauris di Sotto in the mountains. We set off after lunch, on public transport. The final leg of the journey was in an old coach which had a huge engine beside the driver's cab. With a full load we set off at great speed up the steep mountain roads, going round hairpin bends, through tunnels and over bridges, the engine roaring and the driver continually sounding his two-tone horn to warn traffic anywhere around that he was coming through and they should keep out of the way. We arrived safely in time for tea with the family.

The old coach was something like this, I think

Next morning, together with Pierina, Daniela and Sara, we had a walk around their lovely village, then in the afternoon we went with the whole family for a picnic. We drank ice-cool lemo tea in a meadow with views over the mountains

under a deep blue sky, never to be forgotten.

As my time in Italy came to an end, I was now looking forward to getting home. I'd missed Jean a lot and had spent many of my evenings in the church flat writing to her. Often the cook came and tried to talk with me, but he knew no English and would wander off eventually saying *'Povero Jim'* (poor Jim). I wrote ten letters in all to Jean and was looking forward to receiving some back, but they only eventually started arriving in the third week (by very slow air mail).

My final Saturday was spent in the town buying souvenirs and presents to take home, especially with Jean in mind. I made my last visit to Daniela; it had been lovely to spend time with her and I hoped that my visit had been an encouragement to her. In the evening I went to see Mrs Wiles for the last time, as Philip was still away visiting other churches. They were a lovely couple that I was very fond of, and it was a real privilege to have been together.

On the Sunday morning I went to the station to catch the nine o'clock train. Rosario, Peter and Daniela sent me off with the traditional kiss on both cheeks and a British hug, and I started my journey home with mixed emotions of sorrow at leaving and eager anticipation of going home and seeing Jean again.

My journey went well apart from a near hitch at the airport. I still had L1000 in my wallet and decided to look around to see if there was anything I could buy with it. Finding nothing, I went through to passport control, where to my surprise the lady asked me for L1000 airport tax – phew!

I arrived back in a wet cool London which was quite refreshing after all the heat of Italy. I missed my train to Liverpool and had to catch a later one which got me there at three o'clock in the morning! To my delight, Jean and her Dad had come to meet me, and they took me back to their house, rather weary but very happy. I slept the night on the settee in their lounge and spent the next day relating tales of my adventures to them over lots of cups of tea. I was glad I had gone and quite proud I had managed it on my own, but oh! it was good to be home.

Chapter 8:

My time working in the house comes to an end: 1974

So much had changed for me in my four years of working in the house, and my last year was about to bring further changes not only for me but also in the house and church.

Somewhere around this time, I was made a deacon in the church along with Dave

Evernet and Steve Pegg. We were not too sure what this meant and what the responsibilities of being a deacon were. From what we could see in the Bible it was mostly a practical role to look after the elderly and those in need in the church, but we were also called on to do more in the meetings. One effect it had on us was that we had to start having deacons' meetings which took up yet another evening each week. I remember that we took on a number of projects in the church and helped a few folk out. In later years when we had all moved on, Peter Moffat took on the role of Deacon in the church.

In April, Fred Tomlinson went by himself on a visit to Canada. For a while he'd felt that God was going to lead them as a family into ministry abroad, and his one hope though had been that it would be to a country which ate much the same food as we do in England. One of his favourite special meals was fish and chips from Dave's Dingle Diner, so an invitation by friends to go to Canada must have been quite appealing. Some people from the fellowship went to Manchester airport to see him off; he was going to fly on a Freddy Laker Jumbo Jet.

Next day, I took Fred's wife Sheila and the four children, Marty, Andy, Wendy and Sally, along with Fred's Mum, to Anglesey where they'd hired a static caravan for ten days.

A week later, Marty and Andy had to come home for some reason, so I had another trip out there. This time I asked Jean's mum and dad to join me on the day trip, and took the opportunity to ask them for their daughter's hand in marriage – I did this in a cafe in St Asaph! Thankfully, they said yes. Later, Jean told me they really liked me, they thought I spoke nicely and despite me having no money they were happy to have me as a son-in-law.

After ten days, I returned to Anglesey to bring the Tomlinson family home. Jean went to stay with Sheila and the children in the flat in the fellowship house, to keep them company for the remaining week that Fred was away.

Fred returned from Canada with lots of stories of his time there, which he had really enjoyed. He had visited a number of people in Toronto and preached in a few of their churches and had lots of stories to tell. Most memorably, he told us that after the Sunday morning service, many of the congregation went for lunch to a place called McDonald's. Now I had never heard of this restaurant before, so I imagined it to be a posh place with tartan carpets and waiters in kilts!! How wrong can you be!

Around this time, my beloved VW caravanette broke down again. I had nursed it along to keep it going for the last three years. With the help of Dave Fryer, a ship's engineer, we'd had the engine out numerous times, stripped and repaired it and had become experts in putting it back together in a couple of hours. On one occasion when the engine seized up in Exeter on a youth weekend, we'd bought another old VW van which we scrapped and took the engine out to swap it. I think that vehicle had covered many thousands of miles both in the UK and abroad. Sadly, this time I realized it was the end of the road for it. Jeff Clapham took it off my hands to use it as a garden shed.

During a church meeting shortly afterwards, Jean and I were asked to step outside for a few minutes, though we didn't know why. The following morning, I was told the church had made a collection to help me get a new vehicle and I was given £250 (which was quite a lot of money back then).

I had seen a minivan for sale in a garage for about the same amount which I thought would do me, but I had another purchase to make first: I took Jean to a jewellery wholesaler's where she chose a sapphire cluster ring costing me less than £15. She loved it and told me she kept it on a safety pin when she was at work in her nursing uniform. A couple of days later I went and bought the minivan with the remaining money.

Jean and I settled into our normal routine again, trying to get our days off together so we could go on a day trip out to Wales. Sometimes, though, she would have to buy the petrol when I had very little money.

During the following weeks, I'm guessing that

communications continued between Fred and the churches he'd visited in Canada.
Eventually, he and Sheila decided that they would move over there as a family so he could take up invitations for ministry in the Toronto area.

This left the Liverpool fellowship without a leader, so the other elders prayed and then recommended to the church that Paul and Lesley Evans, who were at that time leading a fellowship in Walsall, be asked to come and take on the leadership of the work. On June 23rd, Jean and I went to a wedding down in the Midlands and Paul and Les kindly put us up for the weekend. We had a good time with them, and it was a good opportunity for us to get to know them better.

On Saturday 7th September we held a farewell evening for the Tomlinson family; all the church attended for a final meal together. Next day was their last Sunday with us. The people from the Longcroft Fellowship joined us for the afternoon meeting when, in a rather packed house, we all prayed for them and sent them out with our blessings.

On their final night in Devonshire Road, Fred's

brother Dave and his wife Pat came over from Ripon to say their farewells and Mrs Tomlinson and Jean and I were there too. Far from being sad, we had a happy time with them with much laughter, particularly when the settee Mrs Tom, Dave and Pat were sitting on collapsed – its back legs gave way and they all ended up on their backs with their legs in up the air!

On 12th September the Tomlinson family left for Canada. We hired a double decker bus for the many folk from the church who wanted to go to Manchester airport to see them off.

I had really enjoyed working with Fred. We'd travelled the country together to many preaching engagements, been to conferences, organized days out for the house workers to Wales and days out for the fellowship. We'd laughed together and cried together. Like many in the fellowship, we felt almost part of their family when visiting them in their flat. For me, this was the end of a chapter of my life and the beginning of a new one.

Day out to Conwy, Wales

After they had left, the house seemed very quiet. For a few weeks there was only Brett and I were living in the house till Paul and Les moved up from Walsall. I think John Val was probably in Africa by then, maybe with Keith Kelly and Phil Williamson. John had left his job as a salesman to work full time in the church, much to the disgust of the taxman who took some convincing that he could have actually left such a highly paid job to work for no pay. Peter Gray had left the fellowship house in September 1972 when he married Shelagh Freenes and they went together to help with a mission in Greenland.

Sometime after Fred and family had left, I remember one night in particular. After locking up and going to bed as normal, I got up at two o'clock to go to the toilet and noticed there was a light on downstairs. Opening our flat door and looking over the banister, I could see it was coming from the now empty middle flat. I returned to the bedroom and woke Brett to tell him someone was in the house. He replied 'OK' and went straight back to sleep! So, in fear and trembling, I crept down and slowly opened the door expecting any moment to be attacked by an intruder. To my relief, it was Mr Moffat standing there holding a sleeping bag in his arms. He apologized profusely and explained he had returned from a trip away, and as it was so late he thought it would be easier to stay in the house overnight and had quietly let himself in.

As the time drew nearer for Jean and me to get married, I discussed my future with the elders. I'd been thinking it would be good for me to leave my work in the house, get a paid job and find a place for us to live, which the elders agreed with. In early October, we heard that Phil Woods was leaving his flat in Hadassah Grove off Lark Lane; it was quite small but we thought it would suit us fine so we took it, and Jean went to live there with Pam Tims till we got married. Then I started looking for a job and within a short time Reg Davy managed to get me one on the sales staff in the electrical wholesalers where he worked.

Paul and Lesley Evans moved into Devonshire Road on 28th September. I was still working there for four more weeks, so as to give them a hand with some decorating and helping to get them settled in before I started my new job.

They were given a warm welcome by the church and soon were busy in the running of the house and the pastoral care of a still growing fellowship. They soon became a much-loved couple of the church family. At this point in their lives, they had no children so were able to work together as a couple. With their arrival in the fellowship, inevitably there were a few changes, which worked out well.

They also enjoyed doing fun things with folk. I remember one evening returning from being away, driving down Devonshire Rd and seeing lots of young people running up and down the street. I was not sure what they were doing, but they were having a great time.

After I finished working in the house I continued to live there until our wedding day. Dave Wetherley had moved out previously; I can't remember where he went but I was allowed the luxury of moving into his much larger front bedroom all by myself. On my wedding day, I remember Lesley brought me a cooked breakfast to have in bed. I was a bit nervous of all that was coming so I didn't fully enjoy the food, but it was a lovely gesture of the love and friendship which was to continue and grow in the coming years.

Finally, I want to look at how four years working in the fellowship house had benefited me; what had I learned from it all?

I think I would say I had become more confident as a person. I had travelled quite widely and gained experience from it. Fred had been an encourager to me and many others to become more confident in public speaking and preaching. Although I would say I was not an extrovert, I had enjoyed having many friendships and my life had been enriched as I felt loved by the folk in the church.

I learned a lot about decorating, of course, from just doing it in the house (and also learning how not to do it from watching others when we sometimes had work parties!). This experience was to come in useful in later life as you will see.

I also learned not to make quick judgments about the people who came to our church; as the old saying has it: 'Don't judge a book by its cover.'

The prime example of this was when an old couple started coming to the Sunday meetings. Old Tom and his wife Florey ('Florey love' as he called her) lived in Blackpool in a caravan. He had quite a few front teeth missing and had eyes that pointed in different directions so that you were never quite sure whether he was looking at you or someone else.

They seemed to absolutely love coming to Devonshire Rd Fellowship though, and he would sometimes say about all the folk in the church, 'They're like bees round t'honey pot' in his broad Lancashire accent. Often during the meeting, Florey love would sing a funny little chorus that no-one else knew, 'I'm going up, up, up,' which would bring a few smiles to people's faces. Well, one Sunday he showed up without his Florey love, looking quite forlorn and sad and explained she had passed away during the week. We all felt sorry for him and John Valentine told him to come and stay with us in the house for a while. We gave him a bed in our lounge at the top of the house, and it was sad to see him get up each morning looking so lonely.

The funeral was about a week or so later near Lytham St Anne's, so John, me and maybe Fred or Dave Weatherly accompanied him up there in John's car. We discovered the service was being held in a small country chapel and when we arrived, the young pastor greeted him and surprised us by insisting old Tom should take the service himself.

We thought this was a very strange and shocking thing for him to have to take his own wife's funeral, but it was us in the end who were completely shocked because when the coffin came in, he got up into the pulpit and took that service as if he had been taking them all his life. He thumbed his way through his Bible to all the relevant passages and gave a lovely sermon. We were amazed and extremely impressed. I for one felt I had misjudged him very badly.

After that, we didn't see him for a few weeks, but then one Sunday he showed up again looking very smart in a new suit, sporting a new set of dentures which gave him a lovely smile. He came for a few weeks and then we never saw him again. I like to think he had found a new lease of life and involvement maybe in a church back up there where he lived; I think he still had a lot to give and could be a blessing to many.

So, after four years, with many happy memories to look back on, I was looking forward to what I had hoped for so much: getting married and sharing life with the person I loved.

Chapter 9:

Marriage – the early years

We got married on 18th January 1975. The day started out misty and cold but sunny and thankfully it continued like this for most of the day.

After my breakfast in bed (thank you, Lesley Evans) I spent a quiet morning getting ready. I had been involved in many of our church weddings over the years and normally I would have been dashing round in my van collecting hired crockery, then setting out tables and chairs and doing a hundred and one other things, so it was quite a change for it all to be happening without me.

I think it was quite different for Jean though, as she had to get herself and six bridesmaids ready (yes, six bridesmaids, that's what comes from having so many friends in church!). They were her two nieces, Susan and Helen (daughters of her brother John and wife Ann), her sister Dot, Ruth Morgan, Jane Harrison and Ann.

Brett, my best man, was meanwhile dashing round in his A35 Austin van, collecting flowers and buttonholes from the florist and delivering them to everyone.

Jean had decided that as it was likely to be a cold winter's day she would have her wedding dress and bridesmaids' dresses made from velvet so they would be warm, and she wanted red for the bridesmaids with white muffs to keep their hands warm. They did look lovely on the day, don't you think?

We invited all the church people, my relatives from Birmingham, Jean's relatives and also her friends from the Baptist church where she used to go, plus a few other old friends, so in all Jean had written out over two hundred invitations. We also said children could come too, so it was quite a crowd.

Ron Baker brought Jean and her dad in John Val's car which Sue Withey had decorated, and Roy Jones brought the bridesmaids in his car. The wedding ceremony was held in the Devy

Road house which I believe was full to overflowing. We had asked Norman Meeten to conduct the wedding and speak at it – we asked him to keep it fairly short, but we should have known that would be difficult for Norman!

On the whole, I think most people enjoyed the service, even if it was a bit long, some commenting that they thought the singing was lovely (we did love singing in church in those days and the harmonizing was beautiful).

Afterwards, we posed for photos at the front of the house. Back then, we weren't accustomed to having expensive photographers, but we did ask Jeff Clapham to take the official ones which he did very nicely in black and white. Also, later some of our friends gave us some nice copies of their coloured pictures, particularly Brian Pearson who took some very good ones. During the photo session, the bin men arrived and came into the driveway to empty the bins, which was very unusual on a Saturday. I think they quite enjoyed getting in on the act...

Old Tom showed up as well. We had not seen him for quite a while. He gave us an Isle of

Man 50p as a gift.

The reception after the service was at the Bluecoat Chambers in town. We had some more pictures taken down there and while all the guests were arriving there was a short thunderstorm!

We had decided to have a hot meal at the reception considering that it was winter. This was no small feat considering there was no cooking facilities in the hall, but we successfully managed it. Also, because we had invited children, we had every conceivable fizzy drink available in a wide variety of colours. Jan Horsborough, who was in charge of the catering, got some of her school students to wait on tables and they brought round trays full of them through the reception. Jean's nieces later said they were not normally allowed lemonade because of the effect on their teeth, so on this occasion they took full advantage of the chance to sample every single one of them and got a bit high on the sugar.

We had the obligatory speeches and cards and telegrams read. Jean's dad gave a speech about bone structures which was lovely and very humorous.

By early evening, as the proceedings drew to a close, we said goodbye to friends and family and set off in our minivan for Windermere, where we had a cottage for the week, recommended by Paul and Les. It turned out to be more of a modern house than a cottage, but it was warm and comfortable – and cheap.

After a week of touring round admiring the nice countryside of the Lakes (not a lot was open at that time of year), we went up to Scotland for the weekend, staying at Auchenheath. They kindly made us very welcome, setting up a lovely room for us in the library, with a roaring fire to sit by. While in Scotland, we went up to my birthplace and visited my relatives; as they had not been able to get to the wedding, we took them some wedding cake.

Traveling back on the Monday, we were home by evening where we found all our wedding presents had been delivered to our flat so spent a lovely time opening them all. We hadn't made a wedding list, so it was quite exciting to see what folk had kindly given us. Amongst the gifts was a box of chocolates from someone at the Longcroft, which we thoroughly enjoyed while opening all the rest. It was quite late when we finally went to bed, only to find the sheets full of confetti, courtesy of Les and Paul!

I had the rest of the week off work and we continued converting the flat into our first home. Paul Evans came round and helped paper our bedroom with a lovely yellow flowery paper; Jean's mum made us some curtains on her old sewing machine; we put a lovely deep red wallpaper on one wall in the lounge; I put up some shelves in the very small kitchen to accommodate our wedding present bowls and dishes etc. (I wasn't very good at DIY back then, and the shelves later fell down one night when we had gone to bed, oops!) We didn't have much furniture, so Peter Lock gave us his mother's double bed and I put my mother's bed settee in the lounge along with a comfortable armchair which Keith Kelly gave us (or was it Steve and Joy Pegg?).

Nevertheless, we felt very comfortable and blessed. My bosses from work gave us a spin drier, which was really good of them considering I had only been there a few weeks.

Our little flat was down a narrow unadopted lane which was full of potholes, but had some beautiful old houses and cottages; it was very quaint. We felt very blessed and it was our little bit of heaven (for a while). At the end of my two weeks off, the honeymoon was over and it was back to work.

I've sometimes heard it said that when you're first married you have to allow time for getting used to living together and be prepared to compromise to stay in harmony with each other. Now I can't remember us having any major difficulties along these lines. I think the fact that we both were committed and involved with church, and both had many friends, made us feel very much at home with each other. There was one area though that I had to change.

Back in those days, sometimes in the middle of the night I would wake up with a tickle in my throat. My remedy was to suck a square of Cadbury's Dairy Milk chocolate, which seemed to soothe it. One night soon after we were married, Jean was woken up by the sound of crinkling silver paper and then me sucking away. 'Oh, I can't be doing with that!' said Jean when I explained my problem. I soon discovered that a drink of water solved the problem in more ways than one!

In the ten weeks that I had been working at Lancashire Lamp, I'd had to learn a lot of new things, and had settled into the job fairly well. However, the main thing I learned was that I didn't like shop work very much! (There were other reasons for not liking it too which I will explain later.) The only compensations were that I worked alongside Peter H from church, who was now a good friend and a delight to be with, and with Reg who was a sort of manager – well, that is, he basically ran the show. The only other part I liked very much was when it was time to go home to my lovely wife and the comfort of our little home.

Jean had given up her nursing just before we married, and she planned to help in the Fellowship house in the kitchens etc along with Barbara Peck who was already on the staff. This didn't last for long though, as she soon became very unwell and was sick every day. After a while she went to our doctor, a Jewish man called Cyril Taylor who was the doctor for quite a few of the church folk and enjoyed a bit of banter with us all. I'm sure he enjoyed Jean's visit that day, as the diagnosis was that Jean was pregnant!

The next three months were not so easy for me either. Jean couldn't stand the look or smell of food, and the only thing she could keep down was white fish. My options therefore were to eat white fish every day, or to go into the bedroom with a takeaway.

After Jean's stomach had settled down, our time was taken up with friends coming round for the evening or us going to visit them; deacons' meetings; church; helping friends fix things; and the occasional short stay in Devy Road to mind the house while Paul and Les went away.

While our lives together were very full and enjoyable, there were aspects that were to prove a trial to us. For me it was working at Lancashire Lamp, and for Jean, as the months progressed, it was life in our lovely little flat.

Lancashire Electric Lamp

Lancashire Lamp was a wholesale and retail shop that sold virtually everything electrical, but majored on light fittings, ie chandeliers, table lamps, lamp shades and so on. It had previously been owned and run by a Jewish brother and sister, known as Mr H and Miss S, and in their later years they had sold the business to a city man, I think his name was Mr Smith. I don't think he knew much about the business, so he'd asked them to continue coming in to help him, which they were more than happy to do.

I soon found working there was anything but straightforward. Admittedly, this was before the age of computers! There were five of us in the sales staff whose duties were to serve the customers and fill the shelves, which stocked a great variety of electrical goods behind the counter.

The pricing system was extremely complicated. Most of the prices for the goods on the shelves could be found in huge books on the counter and usually everything else in the showrooms had price tags on them. 'Pretty straightforward,' you would think, except different customers got different discounts. People in trade unions, NHS and the services got 25% discount, while traders and shop keepers got a third off. If you weren't sure, you had to ask Reg. If you couldn't find a price, 'ask Reg' and if you didn't know anything, 'ask Reg' – he seemed to know everything! Reg was a pretty busy man!

Once an order was put together for a customer, it had to be written down in an invoice book with prices for everything, then added up. The total then had to be checked by another member of sales staff (if there was one free). Once confirmed as correct, the total was fed into the till and sale completed. Simple!!

Besides us on Sales, there were two warehouse chaps who were supposed to get stuff from the warehouse for us when customers selected items from display. The warehouse was on two upper floors. The younger of the two men seemed always to be too busy to help, walking around with a clipboard in his hand. The other one was an older chap who sang 'I am the one, you are the B' all of the time, each and every day. He did however make an effort to fetch stuff for you if you found him.

Finally, there was brother and sister Mr H and

Miss S. He was a balding round little man, and she was slim grey-haired lady. They came in every day at ten o'clock and would spend most of the day watching everything that went on in the showroom from the office window. If they spotted anything they didn't like or if we made a mistake, they would come out shouting at us all. Even customers could come in for a sharp rebuke if they were seen touching something, which was against the rules.

On one occasion, Miss S came out the office and shouted down the showroom, 'They're all mad in here!' I was serving a lady at the time and reassured her that Miss S was referring to us and not to her. I did not find this a very pleasant atmosphere.

Things came to a head for me one day after I had been there about a year. Mr H came out to check something at the till and spotted that I had made a mistake for which he told me off and called me 'bird brains.' As you can imagine, I was not happy with that but said nothing. Next day, however, seeing him in the office by himself, I went in and took the opportunity to inform him I was not prepared to be called such names. I think he was taken aback somewhat that I had stood up to him, but I felt justified to have done so.

A couple of days later, though, Reg told me quietly that I should be careful, because Mr H was fuming and was looking for any excuse he could find to give me the sack. I thought that while it would have been good to leave the job and get out, I didn't want to be leaving through getting the sack, so I decided to be extra careful. A few days later, as I was coming back into the showroom after a tea break, I saw Peter coming out of the office and Mr Smith saying to him, 'Thanks for that, Peter.' Later, Reg took me aside again and told me I was safe: Peter had gone in to see Mr Smith on my behalf and spoken up for me, and as a result Mr Smith had told Mr H he would not allow me to be sacked. I think that is true friendship – don't you? Sadly, in later years Peter moved away from Liverpool and we lost touch. I would love to know his whereabouts now.

In the end I worked at Lancashire Lamp for three long years before I finally found another job.

Our trials at home

Our little flat was one of four in a converted house. Above us was an elderly lady who was very nice and kept to herself most of the time. Underneath our bedroom lived an Italian lady who was pleasant; we immediately got on well with her because of our connections with Italy in the past. Underneath our lounge lived a blind lady S and her husband J. They were fine to begin with, but after a few months S started complaining that we made a lot of noise and said that it sounded as if we were dragging something across the floor all the time, which we assured her we weren't. We did however start to make every effort to walk quietly when in the lounge or kitchen.

As the months went on, her complaints seemed to increase, and as Jean was at home more in the day, she started to take the brunt of it all. When later in the year our baby Jennifer arrived, at first she was very happy and liked to 'see' the baby and talk with Jean about her. We needed to have a pram so we asked all the folk in the flats if we could leave it downstairs in the hallway, and everyone agreed. After a while we found out that S would often stand at the front door to smoke and she had started flicking cigarette ash into the pram. You might think this was because she was blind – but we had noticed that when she went out alone she seemed to negotiate her way around without a stick and managed to miss all the many puddles in our unadopted road!!

After this we had to keep the pram upstairs in our flat which was very hard for Jean – when I was at work she had to get it down and pull it back up every day. This situation continued for much of the time we lived there.

Despite these difficulties, life continued. We had friends round in the evenings and had a busy social and church life. I think how busy we were is revealed in an exceptional entry in my diary on 27th October: 'Had an evening in.'

Peter and Sue Moffatt were married on 31st May 1975. They

moved into a flat on Parkfield Road not far from us, and they sometimes came round for the evening, perhaps to play games like Cluedo; on other occasions we visited them. They kindly used to take our washing as we had no washing machine when we were first married.

I was also still working with the other two deacons at church on various projects in the church house or helping out with church members' needs.

Jean's mum and dad came every Tuesday to take Jean shopping to Asda. The only store around then was out in Ditton, nearly ten miles away – a bit different from today! They'd then stay for tea with us when I returned from work.

Despite our trying not to make any noise, we still had S banging on her ceiling regularly, and occasionally she'd make a really loud bang which shook the whole house – we never discovered how she did that!

After a long period of living with this, I came home from work one day to hear S had been complaining a lot and banging the ceiling all through the day and had given Jean a hard time, so I felt I should go down and talk to her. I knocked on the door and S came out. (We hardly ever saw her husband; I think he spent most of his time in the pub.) She started immediately to make complaints about all the terrible noise she'd had to put up with through the day. My reply was, "S, we just want you to know we love you in the name of the Lord Jesus."

Now I don't know why I said this, because I certainly wasn't feeling it at that moment, but that's what popped out of my mouth. The reaction I got was not what I had expected: she went back into her flat and slammed the door and began screaming. Needless to say, it gave me a real fright and left us both shocked. We heard nothing more from her from then on.

We lived in our lovely little flat from January 75 till November 76, when John and Claire Wood told us they were moving from their flat in Peel Street and asked if we would be interested in taking it on. When we went to see it, we liked it immediately. It was a first floor flat, had two bedrooms, a large lounge and a quaint small kitchen three steps down off the lounge. It even had a view of the river Mersey, albeit about 2 miles away across the rooftops.

They recommended us to their Landlord and we had no problem taking on the tenancy and were quick to move in when they left. It took some time getting used to not having to creep round on tiptoe. In the flat underneath us lived a young man on his own, and Jean kept asking him if we were making too much noise. He replied that he heard nothing and not to worry, he worked nights and slept in his bedroom at the front of the house during the day – that was under our bedroom, so he heard nothing. How we thanked God for this flat!!

When we moved out from Hadassah Grove, another of our friends from church took it over. She was a single girl and somehow managed to befriend S from the flat underneath. S eventually confided in her that on the evening I spoke to her, her reaction to what I'd said had really frightened her. Sometime later S started coming to some of our meetings at church, which again was a surprise to us.

Chapter 10: 1976: Glad times and sad times

In the summer of 1976 before we had moved

to our new flat we had a heat wave in June and July which went on for many weeks. Coats were things of the past and it was a matter of trying to find ways of staying cool. At night, we had to sleep with all the windows open and you could hear the crickets in the hedgerows. Sleeping was difficult – we were just not prepared for such weather in England; air conditioning was still a thing of the future and unheard of in cars. There was great demand in our shops for electric fans which were soon in short supply, so most of the customers were disappointed.

We were enjoying many blessings and happy times with our friends. Paul and Lesley were kept busy with pastoring the church, visiting, counselling and running the house on a day-to-day basis, and were much loved and appreciated. Many of our friends were moving on, some to new homes, others to new places, or even to different countries.

Ann Bruce met a wonderful man, Malcolm Alexander and they married in May. Shortly afterwards, they moved into a lovely flat not far from us overlooking Sefton Park. Phil and Barbara Williamson married in July. Fred and

Shelagh and family came back from Canada on June 6th for a month's holiday and it was so lovely to see them all again. I think they spent most of their time visiting family.

In July, I had two weeks' holiday from work and on 3rd July we went over to Ripon for the weekend to see our lovely friends Ken and Liz Whiteway and baby Emma (see photo). The following weekend it was Phil and Barbara Williamson's wedding, after which we went to Skipton for the week. Dave Evernet had bought a small caravan and put it on a site there and was letting fellowship folk use it for free, so we took up the offer. We set off on the Sunday in the Mini van with our Jenny, not yet a year old, on a boiling hot day and – wouldn't you just know it! – the heat wave broke the very next day with thunderstorms and rain. We hadn't thought to take any coats or macs with us and spent much of the week looking for plastic raincoats.

During this time, we faced some sad situations as well. Kathy Rink had started coming to the fellowship around the same time that I came to Liverpool. She'd just come back from Walsall where she had been in teacher training college along with a few other girls from Liverpool.

She was a lovely sweet, quiet girl, and initially when she had returned had come in most days to help Fred and Sheila with their children and any other ways she could in the house. Occasionally she had taken us lads' washing to the launderette for us, which was kind of her. Eventually she got a teaching job in a local primary school.

After she'd been back a few years, she became ill with lymphoma and underwent a major operation to remove her lymph glands. Eventually she regained her health and seemed to be enjoying life again. She travelled a bit, visiting Fred and Sheila in Canada, and learned to ride a bike for the first time. However, after only two years or so the cancer returned in an aggressive form and she quickly became very ill again.

After a short while she came to stay with Paul and Les in the middle flat of number 14, and I remember one day Jean and I took Jenny and called in to see her. I must admit I was quite shocked when I first saw her sitting up in bed looking so weak and frail but she was still cheerful. She loved our Jenny and enjoyed having her sitting on the bed with her for an hour or so chatting and laughing.

Towards the end of June, she was admitted into the old Royal Liverpool hospital where she had her own room. It wasn't very far from where I worked at Lancashire Lamp and when I heard that she found ice lollies were helpful in the heatwave, on one or two occasions I had run out to the shops in my lunch hour and taken some lollies in to her. Despite her weakened condition she remained cheerful and chatty.

Just before we were due to go on our holiday

to Skipton, I called in to see her and explained we were going away for a week; I jokingly told her not to go anywhere while we were away and that I'd be back in a week to see her again. She laughed and said that was unlikely.

We had arranged with Ken and Liz to meet up and have a picnic together while we were in Skipton. When they came, they looked sad and immediately told us that Kathy had passed away on Monday. While there was sorrow in our hearts when we heard the news, we also felt gladness and relief for her that she was now out of her suffering and with the Lord she loved. She was only 29. The funeral was held on Thursday, but sadly we were unable to get to it.

We'd known Kathy's mum for a few years; she was a lovely gracious woman. She had been living in a flat in Garston, but around this time had remarried and moved to Runcorn. We kept in touch with her after Cathy's death and invited her to a few special meetings being held where the gospel of Jesus Christ was explained very simply. After a while she moved back to Liverpool to a flat in a complex for elderly folk near Kensington (I'm not sure what happened with her husband) and she came to a place where she shared the same faith that Kathy had. It was always such a joy and blessing when we were able to visit her.

Eventually she moved away down south somewhere, and I thought that was the end of the story. However, some years later when I was in my decorating business, I got a call from Kathy's sister Lesley who lived in Liverpool. I'm not sure if I'd met her before but I think the link came through someone she'd worked with who was in the fellowship at the time. I understand she was not happy with church and God, maybe because of her sister dying at such a young age.

When I went to see her about the work she needed, she explained she had been unwell for a while and had been off work for nearly two years with an undiagnosed illness, and wanted her lounge decorated. When I started the job, she told me she wanted a "living flame" gas fire instead of the radiant fire she had then. I offered to sell ours to her cheaply as we were finding it was not powerful enough to heat our big lounge and she readily agreed. So, in the process of decorating her lounge, I also opened up her fireplace and fitted our nice fire in.

At the end of the job, I got a gas fitter to come and check it and connect it up. He told me I had done a good job and before he started it up he would just check the flue with a smoke bomb. To our surprise, he discovered the chimney had a serious leak into her bedroom upstairs, and that she had must have been suffering carbon monoxide poisoning for quite some time, which explained her mystery illness. Needless to say, she was very happy to find this out, and so was I, thanking God for an opportunity to be a blessing to her.

During the following year (1977), sadly Mr Moffat became ill and was diagnosed with cancer. He continued in his position as an elder in the church, but was becoming increasingly weak so we saw less of him. However, Paul continued to visit him regularly and kept him up to date with the work of the church. As in Kathy's situation, we prayed much for him but the Lord chose not to heal him, but took him home on 4th October. He was a lovely man and a good elder, very caring and easy to go to with your concerns and problems.

Chapter 11

Parenthood and moving forward

I went over the road to the phone box, not far from our little flat in Hadassah Grove. It was late in the evening of 3rd October 1975, when I nervously informed Oxford St Maternity Hospital that Jean had started having contractions. They advised me to bring her in straight away.

Jean was soon settled in a room all wired up to monitors, and over the next long hours through the night we waited for the birth of our first baby. I kept myself busy by following the advice I had been given in the antenatal appointments, which was to encourage Jean to breathe deeply during the frequent contractions. This was advice which she found quite annoying and unhelpful! I regularly had to tweak the heart rate monitor as it kept getting stuck. Often the nurses sent me to the fathers' room while they examined Jean and sometimes they forgot to let me know they'd finished so I would creep back in hoping I was doing the right thing. At one point I needed the toilet and managed to pull the alarm chord instead of the light switch; that brought the nurses running to see who was in trouble – so embarrassing!!

Through the night a succession of men joined me in the 'fathers' room to wait for the news of the birth of their baby. When the news came through, there would be shaking of hands and congratulations, and then the new father would happily be off to 'wet the baby's head'. However, sadly, this was not so in our case, as labour was prolonged.

By late afternoon the following day, there was concern about the baby's heart rate and we were told a Caesarean would be needed to deliver the baby safely. Once more I was sent to the fathers' room to wait anxiously, but that wasn't for long as I was soon summoned back to her room where I found Jean holding a beautiful baby girl in her arms. All had gone well! I found it quite emotional and a few tears were shed.

Jean was still feeling the after effects of the anaesthetic and said to me, 'Give us a kiss!' and then followed it with 'Oh, I forgot you are a deacon!' Apparently she had also amused the nurses when she came round from the op. When they told her she'd had a baby girl, her reply was, 'Fancy me having a baby girl!' and then she told the Sister, 'Oh, don't you look beautiful in your uniform.' They said they didn't normally get such compliments!

We called the baby Jennifer Ann and like all parents we thought she was perfect.

Over the coming months we discovered just how much we needed to learn about parenting, particularly when all our efforts to get her to sleep at night failed and she cried a lot. We spent hours trying to figure out unsuccessfully whether she was hungry or had wind. After a few weeks of this, I took a morning off work and we went to see Dr Taylor, Jenny lying peacefully asleep in Jean's arms. The doctor smiled at us and said, "Welcome to the world of parenthood!" He suspected Jenny was suffering from colic and told us it would end eventually, and that she was a fine healthy baby. So for the next few months we walked the floor with her and had very little sleep. It's amazing though what you can adapt to, and we survived!

As the months went by, Jenny grew to be a lovely little girl that we enjoyed so much. She fitted in easily with our busy social and church life and was loved by family and friends. Jean's dad loved to call round and take her for a walk in the pram around Sefton Park; he said he felt he had new strength in his legs.

Just round the corner from where I worked in Islington was a little toy shop, and when Jenny was a little older, I couldn't avoid the temptation to start buying her some toys, despite my wages being so low that we struggled to survive: a tin wind-up clown that did a little wobbly walk, then a baby walker with wooden bricks for when she was a bit older

Jean and I with Jenny at Devy Rd

In our little flat there was a small box room with a large window, it was just big enough for a cot, so we decorated it with teddy bear wallpaper and this became her first bedroom.

When we moved to our new flat, Jenny had a proper bedroom all to herself. Our outstanding memory here was of Christmas when she was about two. She loved her dolls, so I had made her a wooden swing crib and along with a few other presents, we left it at the bottom of her bed on Christmas morning. She was still asleep when we went in and we had to wake her. On seeing her presents she immediately jumped out of bed and ran to the window exclaiming, 'Oh, he's gone, he's gone'.

Our financial difficulties continued around this time and we reached a stage when we could no longer afford to insure the van. The solution to this came when Peter Lock was in need of a vehicle, so we lent it to him and he paid for the insurance while we managed without a car.

I had worked at Lancashire Lamp for almost three years and felt it was enough, but what was I to do? The answer came one day when I was talking to Phil Woods who'd previously had our first flat. He told me he had started doing bits of decorating for a few folk he knew, and said he thought I could easily do the same with all the experience I had from working in the house.

I discussed the matter with Jean, and we decided to pray and ask God to supply four houses to paint, then I would quit my job and take up decorating. I don't know why I thought to paint four houses as, although I had plenty of experience of inside work, I'd never painted the outside of a house.

Soon afterwards, Mike and Sue Cadman asked me to paint their house, followed by Norman Meeten saying theirs needed painting, then Jean's dad asked for me to do theirs, and finally somebody living near St Helens asked too – and I'd never even met them!

I immediately gave in my notice and bought a set of wooden ladders and a gallon of turps (a very significant purchase for later on). The lads at work bought me a set of paint brushes as a leaving present. The manager asked if I wouldn't like to stay on a couple more weeks for the trade show which they held once a year and for which we got overtime which was very helpful to us. I didn't have to think much before answering 'No thanks,' and I left very happily. We had a single pound in the bank, so it was very definitely a step of faith. I left Lancashire Lamp on 3rd September 1977.

Chapter 12:

James Hamilton, Painter and Decorator

My first job as a painter and decorator was Mike Cadman's house, a modern semi-detached house on the Wirral. I soon discovered how much I had to learn about painting houses. I found the eaves and gutters were the hardest, as I had to hang onto the ladder at the same time as painting, which I wasn't used to. I think I did a fairly good job, though, for a first effort.

I did however have one mishap. One day, Jean said she would come with me with Jenny who was a lively toddler, then go and visit Ann Vine who lived close by. She didn't want to be too early so stayed with me on the job for a short while, and before she left we decided to have a cup of tea together. There we were, happily drinking tea in the kitchen, when we noticed that Jenny had gone missing. When I stepped out of the back door, there was Jenny, happily painting a foot square of red gloss on the back wall of the house, neatly done with not a spot of paint on herself or the floor, and no doubt feeling immensely proud of herself!

After the initial shock, I set to with my gallon

of turps to try to wash it off. I was reasonably successful, but it still left a stain on the brickwork. I apologized profusely to Mike and Sue that evening when they came home, but to my relief they only saw the funny side of it.

In later life Jenny proved to be good with a brush and helped in the business from time to time, as did all our family when grown up. Jean also proved to be a very good painter at one point and joined me in the business.

When I had finished my first outside jobs (hopefully done reasonably well), I put some adverts in shop windows and got a call from a young Jewish couple (or rather Jean's dad did, we didn't have a phone so he took the calls and came over with the information). They had bought a house in Allerton and wanted all of the interior of their house painted. This was a really good job for me, for beside being a few weeks' work, it also was a gateway into the Jewish community in Liverpool through their recommendations. This gave me opportunity to meet many lovely Jewish people over the years in my decorating career.

One mistake I made on this job was that I found all these little tin tubes on all the door frames in the house from the previous occupants and I proceeded to remove them all before undercoating. When I told the couple what I'd done, they explained to me that according to the Old Testament they were supposed to have a Bible verse on the door frames that they had to touch when going into a room, and that was what the tin tubes contained. (The Bible verse they meant was this: "Write the words of God on the gates and door posts of your house" (Deuteronomy 6:9). Fortunately, the young couple said it was ok because they wanted to replace the tubes with some nicer ones. It was a good lesson learned for the future.

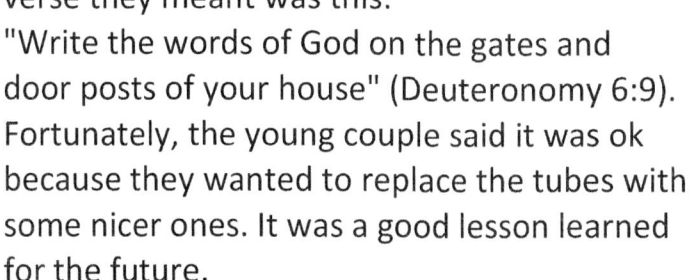

As I neared the end of the job I was running a bit behind schedule, so I asked Terry Murray to give me a hand. He had come to England from Australia and was working in the church house for a while, and he was a very good painter and decorator.

While I was glossing a bedroom window, he started glossing the upstairs door frames and skirting boards then began to work his way down the banisters. I was amazed at the speed of his painting. At the end of the day I had a quick look at his brush to see if there was something special about it! Truth is, I still had a lot to learn, but over the years I got there, through practical experience and through watching Terry on the occasions when he worked with me.

I ran my business for over thirty-five years till I was sixty, working for all sorts of people including doctors, lawyers, a judge – rich and poor. It was a privilege to meet so many lovely individuals.

I did have a couple of slight disasters over the years. Fortunately, I had taken out liability insurance, which was very good at paying out on such occasions. One incident was when I had to strip and re-paper a ceiling in a very nice house owned by a retired doctor. I was having difficulty scraping the off old paper and had to keep spraying the ceiling with water. I had covered everything with dust sheets but when I removed them, I discovered to my horror that the shine on their grand piano had become dull and misty. I got in touch with the insurance company who soon sent in a French polisher who restored it to its former glory, at a cost of £400.

The other time things went wrong was when I was working for an elderly lady. I enjoyed going to her every year to do a room at a time, and this particular year I was to redecorate her open plan lounge. While doing the job, I accidentally managed to damage her carpet very badly while stripping the paint from her banisters.

Once more the loss adjuster was sent out from the insurance company. The lady told me at a later date that she'd had a lovely morning with him chatting over a cup of tea, and he arranged to have her choice of new carpet fitted; she was very pleased with the end job.

Over all the years I worked as a decorator, I very rarely had to advertise. The work seemed to keep coming in through word of mouth, except for one occasion when it completely ran out for several weeks and I had to sign on the dole (the job centre nowadays). I was told I could close my business down for a while till the work came back again, and they offered to get me into college for the time I was off. I chose to study English and Maths. To my surprise, I really enjoyed studying – and unlike my memories of school, the knowledge seemed to sink in this time.

Among the other people on the course was Rachel Hughes who used to be in our church, which was nice, and she started coming again to the services.

Over all the years of decorating we never made a huge profit, but there was always enough to live on and pay the bills and take our family on holidays every year (even if it was only camping sometimes). I think my charges were about average, but I did notice that many other painters worked at weekends, which would have brought in quite a bit more money. I chose to have weekends with the family and to go to church on Sunday, which gave us all good memories to look back on.

I enjoyed the job greatly, not just for the income, but because at the end of it you had made a room or house look lovely – that was the biggest reward for me.

Chapter 13

Neighbours and friends

Living in our new flat was so much better for us and more convenient in so many ways. It was a lot closer to the church house than the old one, which was helpful as we were still heavily involved there. Also, we had space for folk to come and stay with us – friends, family and occasionally other people who were attending the Bank Holiday conferences where Mr North and Norman Meeten spoke regularly.

It was nice too that other friends were living in the same street. In the flat next door was a young married couple who were dear friends to us, Peter and Janet Wilson, who we often had round for supper and who were always willing to babysit for us. Over the road in another flat lived Sue Pollock (later to become Sue Latham) and Chris Davis (later Chris Murray).

Sometime afterwards, when Ron and Anna White got married, they came to live in the flat next door which gave rise to quite a few amusing incidents. One winter, when it snowed, Jean went out to clean all the snow off our Mini van; unfortunately, Ron had a van exactly the same as ours, and it was his that Jean cleaned! Ron suddenly appeared, said a quick thank you, jumped in and went off to work!! One other incident stands out in my memory. Jean and I were on our way to an afternoon meeting. As we emerged from the front door, Ron and Anna also appeared, and at that moment we were concerned to see lots of black smoke billowing up into the sky from behind the flats opposite. Now the fire station was just round the corner at the end of our road, not more than five hundred yards or so away, so Ron and I ran as fast as we could (we didn't have mobile phones then) to inform the firemen. Ron arrived first and was banging away on the door; when I arrived, I saw a doorbell and pressed it. This all brought a fireman to the door pretty quickly, at which point Ron began shouting 'There's a fire, there's a fire,' pointing in the direction of the huge volumes of billowing smoke. He took one look and disappeared back into the building, slamming the door behind him.

We started walking back, rather out of breath, and within a few seconds, two fire engines were racing out of the yard, sirens blaring, the men inside struggling to get their fire jackets and helmets on, and they all vanished up a side street to the scene of the fires. Ron and I followed to see what great disaster we had helped to avert, only to find on arrival it was just an old truck some kids had set fire to!! Needless to say, we made a quick exit and continued on our way to our meeting.

We lived in our second flat for around two years and have many happy memories of it: birthday parties, friends and family visiting, folk for tea or supper.

On one occasion we invited Tom and Louie Orchard for the evening, as they had said they would like to come and visit us. As we sat at our dining table enjoying fellowship while eating, they greatly surprised us by announcing that they wanted to give us their car, a lovely

Morris 1000 Traveller. We were overwhelmed by this gift, but it was very timely for us in more ways than one. Our little Minivan which we loved had started having expensive repair problems. Also, to accommodate Jenny, I had built a wooden frame bolted to the floor in which we'd placed a car seat, but as she was growing now, it wasn't ideal.

The Morris was perfect for us as a family car and also for my decorating, as with the double rear doors it was great for carrying all my decorating equipment. It now enabled us to travel in comfort down to Birmingham to see my sister Grace and family and Jean's brother John and his wife Ann with their two girls in Wolverhampton.

While we were living in this flat, I came across a book by a man called George Dempster, a pastor who worked in the west end of London back in the 1930s during the years of the depression. He became concerned for the numbers of men who were destitute and living in terrible conditions. To discover how he could help them he started going out on the streets, sometimes all through the night, dressed in the same clothes as them to see if he could find some that were willing to receive help. The book told some wonderful stories of how the lives of some of these men were helped and transformed through faith in Christ, and how in many cases families were re- united. I started reading these short stories to Jean at night in bed and we would often end up in tears as they moved our hearts.

One day (it must have been late in the year 1977) I was talking to Paul Evans and told him about this book and some of the wonderful stories. As a result, Paul and I decided we would take a look to see what happened in Liverpool city centre through the night. Peter Buckley said he would come along too.

One cold Friday night, the three of us set off at 10pm, telling only our wives of our intentions. After a couple of hours and finding hardly anyone out on the streets, we were almost giving up but after discussion decided to carry on till 2am (although the thought of warm beds was very appealing.)

Just on two o'clock when we were about to go home, suddenly lots of doors in the buildings all around us opened and many people came out on the streets as the clubs closed. We were amazed, it was just like Liverpool on a Saturday afternoon. We had some Christian literature with us and were soon in conversation with many who were surprised to find us there at this time of night. We had a very busy time talking to them until about 5am, when we eventually managed to get away home for a few hours' sleep.

When the story leaked out, we had quite a few more from church wanting to come with us on the following Friday, and this continued for some weeks with the result that when you looked round the city centre at 3 or 4am, you would find groups of young people all gathered round having talks with us. The police were also there, looking on and wondering what on earth was happening.

Over those years, the church did many forms of reaching out with the good news of salvation through Christ, including some street plays we performed in Toxteth, and sometimes open-air preaching and singing in the town centre on a Saturday afternoon. You might say that we didn't often see results from these efforts but sometimes I think you just don't get to know what effect it has on people's lives.

Several years later, we heard a story that gladdened our hearts. During the time when Len Grates was the leader of the fellowship, he invited a young man who was pastor of a small church mission locally to come and share his testimony and preach in one of our meetings. During his talk he told us of how years earlier his life was in a mess; he was living on drugs and drink and often carried a knife, and basically was messed up by it all. Then, he said, one night, in the early hours of the morning on the streets of Liverpool, a young man approached him and gave him some Christian literature. He took it and put it in his pocket and later read it. This, he said, started him off on a journey which resulted in his conversion and the transformation of his life, an end of his old ways and a new beginning - and now here he was, a new man and a pastor. He then continued to surprise us all by pointing out someone in our congregation who he remembered clearly as the one who gave him the tract that night. This young man went on over the years to become co-pastor of a large church and is now well known in Liverpool.

Chapter 14

Northern Italy earthquake

The 1976 Friuli earthquake, also known in Italy as Terremoto del Friuli (Friulian earthquake), took place on May 6 with a moment magnitude of 6.5 and a maximum Mercalli intensity of X (Extreme). The shock occurred in the Friuli region in northeast Italy near the town of Gemona del Friuli. 990 people were killed, up to about 3,000 were injured, and more than 157,000 were left homeless.

Sometime in early 1978, Salvatore (who had been the pastor of the church in Udine) came to England and paid a visit to Derrick Harrison's fellowship in Birmingham and then on to us in Liverpool.

He told us that after the devastating earthquake, much work had been done in the areas where the earthquake had occurred, but after two years there was still much more needed.

As I understand it, a group of people from a village up in the mountains had made a collection to help a man whose house had been damaged beyond repair. With the money collected they wanted to build him a new home, but with limited funds they needed volunteers to do some of the work. Salvatore's mission on their behalf was to find the volunteers.

Being self-employed, I was in a good position to get involved so Jean and I agreed to go, together with several others from the Liverpool area and some from Birmingham. The party included our Jenny, Pete and Sheila Gray with their two boys, Terry Murray and Chris Davis (later Murray). Dave Wetherley and others from the Liverpool area came on a later date with Derrick and Barbara Harrison and another group from Birmingham.

At this time, John Valentine had been planning an overland trip to Africa and was looking for some VW vans to use for the trip. One day, we saw one advertised and Jean and I went along with John to see it. It was a left-hand drive red VW mark 2 van with side windows but nothing inside. John and I took it for a test drive leaving Jean with the seller, who on discovering that Jean had been a nurse, proceeded to show her the scar on his abdomen from a recent operation – not that she particularly wanted to see that!

The van seemed to run all right so John bought it and we thought we might be able to borrow it for our trip to Italy. Soon after purchase, Dave Fryer and I inspected the engine more closely and to our dismay discovered there was a rattle which seemed to suggest that there was some wear in the main bearings. Undaunted by this, we set to and took the engine out, and Dave and I stripped the engine down in the basement of no 16. For those technically minded, we had the crankshaft reground at nearby Newtons Motors and with new bearings put it all back together. To our shock and great disappointment, we then discovered, after all this work, that it was the crank case which was worn; all our work was in vain. The only recourse now was a new engine, which John and I purchased in Manchester at a cost of around £700. We did all this on the day our journey to Italy was due to start. In the meantime, while all this was happening, Derrick Harrison had asked John if the Birmingham group could use the van for the trip, so we had to find another vehicle to travel in. Fortunately, we managed to find someone who had a Land Rover they could lend us.

In the end, it worked out well for us to travel in the Land Rover, as we could start on the appointed day, 10th July. After tea, we loaded the vehicle with all our gear (it had a full-length roof rack) and left for Ramsgate at nine pm.

Before we set out, Jean and I were given two gifts totalling £150 to help cover some of the costs. This helped us a lot. Also, just before setting out, someone else in the fellowship told us to go and fill the Land Rover with petrol and they would pay for it – now Land Rovers have a very big fuel tank and we had a couple of jerry cans too, so that was a substantial gift!

Finally, we set off that evening to drive down through the night, three in the front and the rest, including three children, in the back on the two side bench seats. Land Rovers aren't the most comfortable vehicles but we managed all right; I think the children slept on the floor down the middle in sleeping bags. I took the final stint at the wheel in the early hours of the morning, with Sheila staying awake to feed me boiled sweets to keep me going till we arrived in Ramsgate at 6.00 am ready for the early morning hovercraft at 7.15. It was a nice morning so we had time to stretch our legs in the sunshine before boarding. During our walk, our Jenny (now two and a half) had a fall and split her lip, which was a bit traumatic, but we managed to sort it out before driving onto the hovercraft.

This was an interesting experience for us all. We left the Land Rover in the middle of the craft and were shown to some comfortable seats which were down each side of the craft and were soon on our way speeding quite smoothly over the waves. It proved to be quite a comfortable fast journey over to Calais.

Once on French soil, we travelled south through the day reaching Châlons-en-Champagne at 5.30, where we planned to find a campsite for the night. We had brought Peter Gray's large tent which had four compartments so we would all fit into it okay.

However, just as we were going through the town, one of the half shafts in the back axle broke.

Fortunately, the Land Rover also has front-wheel drive so we were able to switch over and continue on till we found a campsite. It's also fortunate that we had two spare half shafts with us as it's well known that they are a weak spot in Land Rovers and easily break. After tea Terry and I went back into the town where we found some friendly folk who offered to help us to get it fixed in the morning.

I think we had a reasonable night's sleep considering we were all in one tent, and we were up at 8 in the morning. During breakfast, a young man called Francis appeared and Terry went off with him in the Land Rover. We all had to sit around for the rest of the morning anxiously hoping and praying they would be able to fix it. It was with some relief that at 1 o'clock we saw Terry driving back onto the campsite with a big smile. I think the fellows who did the repair must have understood we were on a mission and didn't give us a bill for the work; however, Terry did give them a few francs as a gesture of thanks.

We soon packed up and were on our way again, but we only managed five hours' travel that day until we needed to stop to set up camp for the night and to have our evening meal. We camped in a town called Gray, I think because Peter fancied staying in a town with his name.

Next morning, we needed some bread and milk for breakfast so I went off to the camp shop with Chris, who was the only one among us who could speak a bit of French. Poor Chris, when it came to asking for our needs she became suddenly shy and couldn't think of the names of what we wanted, so we stood there feeling a bit embarrassed until I thought to ask for it in Italian which has some similarity – latte and pane instead of lait and pain – and which they seemed to understand.

Leaving Gray at 10 am, we crossed into Switzerland and stopped for lunch at Lausanne on the banks of Lake Geneva, then on to Sion where we camped in some woods. The following morning, we were on the move again by 11.00 am and went over the Simplon pass, stopping for lunch at the top where we found some snow, then on down the other side, crossing the Italian border at around 3.00 pm and we had tea next to Lake Maggiore. I think by this point we had grown weary of setting up camp, so with common consent we decided to travel on through the night crossing the north of Italy, and finally, after a couple of hours' rest and a bit of a snooze, we reached our destination of Torreano de Martingacco, a village near Udine.

Now we only had an address but no instructions on how to find it, so we found a bar and I went in with Sheila (I think) and asked for directions. One of the local men proceeded to give me directions in Italian with me saying 'Ah, si, si, grazie.' As we returned to the Land Rover, Sheila asked me what he'd said and I had to confess I hadn't a clue – I've never been any good with my Italian rights and lefts. So we set off again, trying to guess what the instructions had been, only to find ourselves back in front of the bar again after about ten minutes. This time the gentleman kindly came out and led us about a hundred yards further on to a lane on the right, down which we found the villa where Salvatore lived and where we were to stay for the next few weeks.

We discovered on arrival that Salvatore had left the church in Udine and was now working for a local radio station doing religious broadcasting, and he was living in this rather nice modern villa. It had some land behind it and he had managed to acquire several small caravans which would be our homes for the next few weeks so we were quite comfortable.

Our first day there was restful, then in the evening we had a meeting in the large lounge in the villa when Salvatore spoke, with two more meetings the next day, Sunday. In between meetings, we took our first trip into Udine to visit Daniela, Sara and Pierina. It was lovely to see them again, and Daniela was now married.

We spent Monday morning changing money at the bank and registering ourselves at the town hall, then having the afternoon free, we decided to head for a beach at Bibione where we had a relaxed and enjoyable time, swimming and having a picnic. It was here that I first noticed a friendship beginning between Terry and Chris, after they had gone for a swim together and ended up standing in the sea, talking for rather a long time.

Next day, we were up very early and set off at 7.30 am for a mountain village called Forgaria nel Friuli. It took us over an hour to get there, with some of the route winding up a steep mountain road. We had been told that our job was to build a new house from scratch, beginning with the foundations.

On arrival on site we found the old house was still standing, very badly damaged by the earthquake and unsafe to enter, so we had to hang around for a few hours till a digger and lorries turned up at 11.00 am and proceeded to knock the house down and remove the rubble. All we could do that day was erect a wire fence to stop stones and boulders rolling down the hill and thereafter watch the proceedings, until it was time to do our steady return journey. There was little we could do for the rest of the week, which was a bit frustrating. Terry and I went to the home of a lady living in a place called Buia and did a little painting for her, interspersed with some interesting chats (I think in English).

Sometime during this week, the other party arrived from Birmingham. This included Derrick and Barbara Harrison, Dave Wetherley, Alwyn and Janet Griffiths from Stourbridge (Lesley Evans's uncle and aunt), and Andrea from the Longcroft (who'd only been a Christian for a short time and thought everything was absolutely wonderful).

Finally, on the Saturday we were able to go back up the mountain to start work on the house by beginning to dig out the foundations (by hand), which we did for the following few days. It was very hot, hard work and our morning break was so welcome when we were brought cans of cold Coke to quench our thirst. Some of the ladies, including Jean and Sheila with the children, came along too to help with preparation of meals in the local village.

As you can see in the photo, we had a mammoth task as we had to dig down into the rocks to make a solid foundation.

On the Sunday, we were invited to the village where people had raised the money, and were treated to a nice lunch; the wine was flowing freely, every time our glasses showed a little space they were refilled. We were not used to drinking wine so some of it went under the table, but we learned eventually to leave our glasses fu

Monday
out the f
Wetherle
shutterin
poured.

Back at the villa, we had all our meals outside which was very pleasant.

During the following week, the digging was completed and the shuttering went up, and we made the steel frames for re-enforcing the foundations and carried them into the trenches.

When all was ready, the concrete mixer lorries wound their way up the mountain at regular intervals and started pouring concrete into the trenches and shuttering.

One day we were just packing up to go home when we were told there was another load on the way, so we settled down to wait for it to arrive, which it did eventually after dark. It took a while to unload, so it was quite late by the time we were on our way back down the mountain in the Land Rover.

When we finally got home our first thought was to get the children to bed. Dave

Wetherley was most concerned for us and told us to have a lie in in the morning instead of our usual early morning drive to the site. In the evening Derrick and Barbara came to our caravan to discuss the situation. We were concerned for the women and children who were coming up with us each day, which meant them getting up very early each morning, and also for Dave Wetherley that the work was too heavy for him. We decided we should approach Salvatore about it all.

While we were discussing it, who should pop in to see us but Salvatore himself and there was a rather embarrassing silence until he left. Anyway, he did agree with our proposals and from then on the ladies stayed down at the villa while we worked up on the job. Dave Wetherley was given a job in the villa grounds of building a chicken coop.

Up in the village where we had lunch each day (our little Jenny in the foreground age 2½). Note Dave Wetherley on top of the Land Rover.

Things didn't quite work out for the better for the ladies as we had hoped. They were given lots of chores to do in the villa and also Salvatore had discovered that Jean could bake the most wonderful apple pies, so while everyone else was having their afternoon siesta, Jean was slaving away baking in a hot kitchen. She was not too happy.

One evening later that week, Jean and I took Dave Wetherley out to a local bar to have a little light relief from it all, and over hot chocolate we had a good laugh. asked Dave how he was getting on with the chicken coop, and he replied it was hard work because the wood he had been given was "fowl."

We did get a day off each week and had a few trips out, one to Venice which was nice.

On another occasion, Daniela invited us to visit her family up in their mountain village, Sauris de Sotto. This didn't go terribly well though, as there were a lot of traffic jams and by the time we got up to the village, we only had about an hour or so to look around and then had to start back again. However, it was interesting to be shown around the family business of preparing hams and cured meats.

One day, Salvatore asked me if I'd like to go with him to see the radio studios where he worked, so I had a nice trip into Udine with him and a tour round the radio station. On the way back he surprised me by asking if Jean and I would consider coming out to join them in the work there in Udine. Much as I love Italy (and much to Jean's relief), I declined the invitation. I may be wrong, but I wonder how much Jean's apple pies influenced his desire to have us out there!

Towards the end of our time there, we saw the work progress from the foundations being laid to the shuttering going up for the walls and then the concrete mixers coming up to fill them.

On Monday of the last week, we went for the last time to Fogaria. Next day, Terry and I went in to Udine and did some decorating in Pierina's flat. On the Wednesday, we decided to take a trip into Yugoslavia in the morning, because as well as it being a nice place to visit, the petrol was very cheap there.

Unfortunately, we had forgotten to take the green card (insurance) so at the border, the stern Yugoslav officials wouldn't let us in, so it was rather a wasted trip.

In the afternoon we sorted all our gear and packed it onto the Land Rover. In the evening, we had a meeting till 9.00 pm when we went in to visit Daniela, Sara and Pierina and we didn't get back till midnight. We didn't know it then, but that was the last time we were to see them for nearly forty years, as in the busyness of life and circumstances we sadly lost touch.

Thursday, 10th August, after having been there for four weeks, we set off for home at 9.00am. We decided to return a different way, through Austria, Germany and Belgium. By 5.00 pm we reached Salzburg and camped for the night. Next morning, we left at 9.00 to go into Salzburg to visit the Mirabell Gardens to do a little dancing and singing ("Doh a deer, a female deer"), then went onwards to camp in Germany before our final drive up through Belgium.

We decided to go straight through to the ferry terminal rather than camp again. We hoped we could get on an earlier ferry than the one we were booked on next morning, so we got there at 2.00 am and thankfully we found that was fine, as there was plenty of room on the ferry, we were to simply go and join the lines of cars, ready for the next ferry which might be in about 20 minutes time.

Once stopped, we thought it would be nice to get out and stretch our legs and get some fresh air as it was quite warm. We had hardly been there ten minutes when suddenly the lines of cars started moving forward so we quickly returned to the Land Rover, only to discover that Terry and Chris were missing.

We hadn't noticed them go off so had no idea where they were. We quickly set off in search leaving someone to look after the children in the Land Rover. I thought they had probably gone off to find a nice quiet romantic spot, maybe overlooking some water. I soon found a stretch of water, perhaps a canal, and followed it along for a short distance. Then I saw a bridge and on looking up, sure enough, there they were, arm in arm. Panic over, we were soon all back to the Land Rover. And that was the beginning of a lovely couple's relationship which culminated in their marriage.

We joined the other vehicles boarding the ferry and continued our journey through the night finally arriving back in Liverpool on Sunday morning at 11.30, right in the middle of the morning service. The church folk saw us arrive and were so excited that despite having been up all night, we joined them for a while to let them know how we had got on. We were glad though to go home as soon as we could to get some sleep.

The following day, Monday, we drove over to Cliff College where the summer conference was being held. Jean's nieces joined us there while her brother John and his wife Ann went off on holiday together. They camped with us for the week in our tent. Jean recalls that they enjoyed going on all the trips out with the children's clubs each day. My sister Grace and her husband John came for the week as well with their children.

My 1978 diary shows some changes from previous years', I think mostly because I was self-employed and running a business, so most of the entries were to do with who I was working for and what the jobs were, and not so much about our church and social life.

One more entry is of interest though, and stands out in my memory. On Thursday 28th October, I'd been painting the outside of a house on the Wirral when at lunchtime it began to rain heavily and was windy too. I packed up all my gear and went home and said to Jean, "Let's go to Scotland and camp for the weekend." Jean said she was up for it so we threw all our camping gear into the back of our Morris Traveller and the three of us set off for Scotland.

On the way out of Liverpool, we called in to Jean's mum and dad to let them know where we were going, and they kindly gave us some money to stop at a B&B on our way up. That was just as well, as it was such a terrible night with wind and heavy rain, and we also had a puncture on the way and had to get it fixed. We managed to get near to Glasgow when we found a B&B with a room for us all to share, but we had to have our breakfast in the kitchen as they were full (it was a very tasty cooked breakfast).

Next morning, we drove on to Glasgow where we popped in to see an uncle and auntie before going to Loch Lomond. The weather continued to be cool, windy and showery, but we found a nicely sheltered spot in a camp site near to where I had lived when young. It was an area where Grace and I had played, there was a stream running down through the middle which we'd splashed through and dammed, so it was lovely to see it again.

At that time, we still had my four-man ridge tent with no inner so it could be a bit draughty, but in the evening we put our hot water bottles in the sleeping bags and drove out to Luss with the car heater on full blast, had hot chocolate drinks and came back to have a good night's sleep.

On the Saturday morning, the weather was better, and we have an 8mm film clip of me playing football with Jenny while Jean is cooking a bacon breakfast in the tent doorway. After that, we went to Balmaha and then a boat trip up the loch in the afternoon. In the evening we went to visit my auntie Minnie and had some supper with her, then back to the campsite for another good night's sleep.

On Sunday, we packed up and had a ride round to Helensburgh, then went on to Auchenheath Fellowship late in the afternoon, where we met up with friends. We stayed overnight with Jock and Liz where we had a lovely time, before starting our return journey the following day, 3rd October. Thankfully, the weather improved on our return home and I finished the job painting the outside of the Wirral house the next day.

There were many other things that happened during 1978 which sadly I didn't record in my diary. I think this is because my main focus was now on running my decorating business. Besides our usual stream of visitors and visits to friends and often going to see Jean's mum and dad on Saturdays, I did record a couple of other important dates:

John and Celia got married on 24th June and on 1st July, Steve and Joy Pegg left for mission work in Papua New Guinea. This was the beginning of a life in mission for them, later in the Philippines, where I understand they have been a great blessing to many.

Also, on 14th October my diary tells me we had a farewell evening for a group going to Nigeria (yet to find out who they were). The rest of the year continued uneventful, except it turned to be quite a cold snowy winter. We were a very happy contented little family and thankful for the many blessings we had.

Jenny's third birthday party

As we approached a new year, we had no idea that we were about to enter a new and unexpected chapter in our lives.

Chapter 15

Bryn Goleu, Lanfairfechan

Around this time, we had been praying about our future and had told the Lord we were wanting to do His will, whatever that meant for our lives. So 1979 unexpectedly turned out to be an eventful year for us.

Firstly, the year started by being very cold with snow which continued pretty well until 20th February. Secondly, I ran out of work!!

My diary for the first week shows how difficult that new year period was:

Heavy snow.
No work that week and none in my order book. I had to go to the Job Centre ('on the dole' as it was called in those days) and sign on. I also had to claim housing benefit to pay our rent.
Not feeling well, bad cold.

Tried to get petrol but none was available because of a strike of tanker drivers. Freezing day.

The next two weeks continued much in the same vein, doing some decorating in our own flat and helping with bits of work at the fellowship house, intermixed with going along to some meetings around Liverpool – one of them was with Paul Evans, John Wood and Dave Stewart to a Christian Union meeting at C F Mott College.

Then on Friday 19th our doorbell rang at 8.45 am. I still had no work and we were not expecting anyone so we'd not been in a hurry to get up as it was snowing and cold. I must have put on my dressing gown to go and answer it. To my surprise and slight embarrassment Paul and Les Evans were on the doorstep. I'm guessing that we quickly dressed and made them a cup of tea.

Once settled round our table, we soon realised that they had not come for a social visit but had something to discuss with us concerning another fellowship. Dick and Sylvia Hussey had returned from Spain several years earlier and had moved to North Wales, taking up an invitation to start a fellowship in a large house called Bryn Goleu, in Llanfairfechan (along the coast halfway between Conwy and Bangor). We didn't know a lot about it, other than that a few families from our church had moved there to live in the village and join them. I had been to the house a couple of times on some sort of business during the years when I was working at Devonshire Rd fellowship house, but all I had seen of it was the main hallway inside the front door and a staircase with a magnificent stained-glass window half way up.

The situation Paul and Les now presented to us was that Dick and Sylvia felt the Lord was leading them to go back to Spain and they were looking for someone to come and run the fellowship house. I believe several others from different groups had already been approached but didn't feel able to accept the invitation. Paul told us that in discussion with Norman Meeten, they had both thought of us, leading to the unexpected call that morning. He asked if we would consider moving to North Wales for a year or so to take on responsibility of the work there with support from the Liverpool fellowship. We were a bit taken aback but open to the suggestion. Paul said he would arrange a time for us all to go over and see how we felt about it.

In the meantime, I still didn't have much work so continued to do odd jobs at home, and the snow kept coming! At the end of January, I went over to Walsall for five days of work at Lesley Evans' mum and dad's house. Leaving Jean and Jenny behind at home, I travelled down one Monday morning and managed to complete the work in five days so returned on Friday evening still in very snowy weather.

In the following week I went to Devy Rd to help Peter Moffat put the engine back into the red VW van. (This van had broken down on our return trip from Italy – Dave Fryer thought there was a slight oil leak which damaged the engine. Somehow the van had found its way back to Liverpool where we repaired it.)

On Sunday 11th February, after the morning meeting, we went with Paul and Les to visit Dick and Sylvia at Bryn Goleu. At that point, we hadn't mentioned anything to family or friends at church, as we needed to see what the situation was first.

On the Monday morning Dick showed us around the house and grounds and we spent some time talking with him about the running of the house. We were introduced to the house's owner, Mam Bailey (Mam means 'mother' in Welsh), who had originally invited the Husseys to go there. She seemed a nice old lady in her 80s, rather disappointed that Dick was leaving, but reasonably happy that we were coming to take over. The same evening, we went to visit Pam Nuzum who lived with her parents in a nearby village, Aber, at the time.

On Tuesday morning we started out for home again after an informative visit, stopping in Llandudno for lunch, and arriving home at 5.30. There was a church business meeting arranged for 9.00 that evening when we brought the situation to the church. Jenny had to keep the secret with us till it was revealed!

The following Sunday, we had another business meeting when it was decided that yes, Liverpool Fellowship would take on the responsibility for Bryn Goleu, and the Hamilton family would be leaving Liverpool and moving to Bryn Goleu to take over the work!! I think our feelings were a mixture of excitement and 'what have we let ourselves in for?'

For the next three weeks we went over to Bryn Goleu each weekend with different people coming along with us. I think this was because Dick was visiting different churches each Sunday to preach, and we had to fill in for him while he was away. One weekend in early March we were invited to visit John and Sue Lonergan in their little cottage on the sea front, where we had a nice afternoon and felt very much at home with them; they were a very lovely young couple we thought.

The photo shows Bryn Goleu as it is today, not much changed from then.

In the final weeks of March, various people including Marg Burrell and Enid Harrison came to help us pack our things for moving. I removed various cupboards I had installed in our kitchen, and put them up in Jean's mum and dad's house where Peter Gray, Dave Fryer and I had been doing a kitchen upgrade.

Our date for moving was the beginning of April. Sunday 1st was our last Sunday in the Devonshire Rd church, when we were prayed for. The following Tuesday, Peter Moffat hired a large van which we loaded with all our possessions, and we arrived in Wales in the late afternoon. Dick and Sylvia were still not ready to leave so we had to store all our stuff in the garage and we lived in one of the bedrooms for three weeks till they departed. During that time, Liverpool Fellowship had a tent crusade so we came back to help with that for almost two weeks before returning to Llanfairfechan. Finally, it came to the time when Dick and Sylvia were leaving. On Sunday 22nd April we held a valedictory service for them. Horeb, one of the large non-conformist chapels in the village, was hired for the service and many people travelled from various places to come to it, including a coach load from

Liverpool. Pastor North came to speak and pray for them. Afterwards a lunch was prepared for everyone back at Bryn Goleu. We were able to meet many of the fellowship people from the surrounding area, but when they were leaving after lunch, quite a few said to us that it was nice to meet us but they didn't feel to join us from then onwards, now we were taking over the work in Bryn Goleu. I don't think I blamed them; after all, we were just a young couple from another church, unknown to many of them, and over the weekends we had been coming across we'd probably run the meetings differently from how they were previously.

The one exception though was John and Sue Lonergan (see photo), who told us they would like to continue with us. We were delighted and very relieved at this, not only because they were a lovely couple to have with us, but also Sue was a good piano player and John was able to preach sometimes in the services.

Later in the afternoon we waved off all our friends from Liverpool in their coach and we were left with Paul and Les, Mr North and John and Sue and of course Mam Bailey. That evening, we had our ordination service where they prayed for us. It turned out to be a very small meeting….

Dick and Sylvia had planned to leave the following week with their two youngest children, but their car had a fault and had to be repaired at a garage in the next village, Penmaenmawr, where the mechanic, John (a lovely Christian man) was doing the repairs. While the Husseys were still with us, Dick explained a few details of how things worked in Llanfairfechan. For instance, the milkman Aled ('Jones the Milk') would deliver whatever milk we needed each day if we left a note out for him; 'Jones the Coal' would order smokeless fuel for the Rayburn; and if you had letters to post, you could leave them in the window of the porch and the postman would take them when he delivered the letters to us. (I never found out if he was 'Jones the Post'!)

We also learned where they bought all the supplies for the house – a Cash and Carry near Deganwy, a frozen foods warehouse, and the big Asda in Llandudno – and were told how to get there using all the back roads to evade the traffic jams which frequently occurred at that time before the new A55 road and Conwy tunnel came through.

When the car was repaired, Dick and Sylvia along with their two youngest children, Richard and Evangeline, finally left for Spain, leaving their middle son John with us, as he wanted to finish his secondary schooling in Bangor and had the promise of a job with a local farmer which he wanted to take up. Their two eldest children, Charles and Grace, were already living down at Rora House in Devon. Paul and Les agreed to be John's legal guardians, although in practice it was Jean and I who took on the task of caring for him, which was a pleasure for us. About two years later we had to go to a parents' evening at his school, not long after we'd had our second child, Peter, who was with us in the pram, and we attracted quite few puzzled looks as we lined up to see each of his teachers.

Now we were able to move in properly. Over the years that the Husseys had lived there, quite a lot of work had been done in the attic space, which I understand was originally just a large area mainly suitable for storage. With the help of folk like Derek Spriggs and Peter Gray and many others, it had been converted into bedrooms and other rooms, dormer windows were added, and it also had a proper staircase leading up to it. This floor became our home along with other staff members who were soon to join us; John Hussey also had his bedroom up there with us all, and it was very comfortable. There was a largish lounge at the front which we used mostly so we could have family times together.

My feelings at the time, once we were properly moved in, were a mixture of excitement and amazement. Our heart's desire was to serve the Lord and be a blessing to others, but on top of that we had moved from a flat in Toxteth, Liverpool 8 to a beautiful big house in a seaside town surrounded by lovely countryside! I guess the realisation was yet to come that there was also to be a lot of hard work involved.

In discussions with Paul, we figured that as there was not much of a church work to start with, maybe the best way forward was to open the house for folk to come to us for church weekend breaks, church conferences and retreats, and for individuals coming for a break etc.

On the next weekend after we were just settled in we had our first group, when 30 young folk from C F Mott College came for a weekend conference. It was our first attempt at catering for a group but Pete and Joy Palmer (who had moved up to Liverpool from London to help Paul in the eldership) had come over for the weekend, and Joy was very encouraging and just said to Jean, 'Come on, I'm sure we can do this together,' (and they did, very successfully).

Not long after this Myrtle Jones and Jan Richardson joined us on the staff, and we were soon working well as a team looking after the various guests who regularly followed on from our first weekend. We were not registered as a guest house so made no charges for those who came to stay, but rather trusted that they would leave a gift that would cover their visit. In general, this worked okay, I think there were only a couple of exceptions in all our time there when someone never thought to leave anything. This money gave us enough to run the house, and also take a small percentage for all of us on the staff to have a bit of money too.

As we settled in over the next few weeks, we started to realize more about the situation we had moved to. Originally, I'd wanted to continue in much the same way we were used to in Liverpool. For instance, we had just come from a two-week tent crusade and I wanted to continue to tell people about the love of God and the good news of Jesus, but I felt the Lord say to me to just stay quiet and try to be friendly with folk. We soon found out why this was. We noticed that when we went to the shops in the village, the locals would look at us suspiciously, and we were aware they were talking about us in Welsh, so we didn't know what they were saying.

Eventually, we discovered that in general the English were not always popular, and also they thought of Bryn Goleu as some sort of religious community, something mysterious they didn't know much about, in the big house on the hillside. (Much later on we also discovered they had a misconception about a simple little thing we did every day. In the mid-morning and afternoon, we rang a loud handbell outside to tell people maybe working in the grounds it was coffee or tea break time. The locals believed this to be a call to prayer!)

It took quite some time to overcome the reserve that the locals had towards us, but when it came, it happened in quite an unusual way, which I'll come to later.

Mam Bailey

Mam Bailey on her ninetieth birthday with two of her daughters

Our other learning curve was concerning Mam Bailey. We knew very little about her but we grew to love her very quickly. Her routine each day was to sit in the morning room in the middle of the ground floor, where there was a Rayburn stove which was kept burning all the time. She had her special chair right next to it, where it was always comfortably warm, and the room was the hub of the house where we sat during the day for our breaks and to talk.

Here, Mam would watch all that was going on through the day and chat with any who had time to sit with her. One day Jean asked if she would like to go with her in our Morris Traveller to do the weekly shop around Llandudno. She really enjoyed her trip out and said it had been such an adventure going up over the Sychnant Pass into Conwy and on round the various warehouses and shops to get all the stores for the following week, then back over the pass again which was very narrow and steep. She said afterwards it had been so exciting and she had really enjoyed it.

Only a few weeks after this Mam collapsed one morning when downstairs and had to be carried up to her bedroom. At the time we had our friend Ann staying with us and together the four girls struggled to get her upstairs and into her bed. We called her doctor, who was soon with us and diagnosed her as having a very weak heart and suggested she should stay in bed from now on and be cared for. It was fortunate that Jean and Myrtle were both nurses, and together with Jan who quickly learned all that was necessary, they tenderly and lovingly looked after her each day from then on. Dr Bellis, who was a lovely man, said he would come every month from then on to keep a check on her, which we were very agreeable to. (Later, when Mam's daughter Joan came to live in Bryn Goleu too, she used to bake bread every week, and Dr Bellis always left after his regular visit with a broad smile and a fresh loaf tucked under his arm!)

My daily routine changed now. After breakfast I would go and spend the first half hour chatting with Mam, reading scripture with her and having a time of prayer together. It was here that I started to learn much more about her. She told me that her parents had also had a strong Christian faith and had wanted their lovely house to be used for the Lord. They often had missionaries come to stay with them when home on furlough, and she recalled that when she was a young girl they had the famous cricketer and missionary C T Studd come occasionally, whom she nicknamed Uncle Scallywag because he used to tease her and play tricks on her.

Mam married a builder and I'm guessing they eventually took over the house from her parents, but he had passed away some years earlier, though I'm not sure when. He had been a widower with three children, and then they'd had three daughters as well. Julia lived in Dwygyfylchi near the Sychnant Pass with her husband Jock Hamilton (no relation to us).

Julia was the manager of the local Little Chef and Jock was the head chef for the Little Chef chain of restaurants and produced the menus for them all. Another daughter, Joan, lived in Devon with the Exeter fellowship, and Margery lived down south somewhere with her husband.

The first of the family we met was Julia, who became a regular visitor along with her own daughter to see her now bed-bound mother, and later on a call came from Margery who wanted to come up with her husband for a few nights. As this started to unfold we realized that Bryn Goleu was not just a fellowship house, but was also still the Bailey family home, and when we got to know the rest of the family we told them they should feel free to come any time. We told Margery and her husband we would always keep a room for them to stay with us (hoping they would not come in mid- summer when we were especially busy!).

And so that's how our time in Bryn Goleu began and slowly expanded. Our small meeting started to grow as more people joined us from the locality. Some of them had been part of the fellowship in the past; for instance, Wayne and Greta came from Penmaenmawr, a lovely couple who also became good friends to us. As time went on, we met various others from the area and our meetings started to get larger.

Sometime later, a couple from Colwyn Bay, Brian and Tegwen Rainford, started coming and were to become a significant part of the fellowship in later times.

In the first weeks up until July 1979, mostly we had friends come over from Liverpool, and also we who were working in the house invited our families to come and stay with us for a few days at a time. It was lovely to meet Myrtle and Jan's parents and also super that we could have my sister Grace and her husband John and children, Jean's mum and dad and Aunty May, Jean's sister Dot and later on Jean's brother and his two girls. It gave us opportunity to spend time with them and to take them for days out in the countryside.

On one occasion we had all of my family and all of Jean's family together and we went for a day out to Bodnant Gardens. While there we found a very large bench which we all managed to sit on and got someone to take a picture of us all which we treasure to this day.

Also, Paul and Les were regular and welcome visitors. I think it gave them some relief from the busyness and stress of running a busy house church in Liverpool and Paul enjoyed doing work in the gardens to relax. We had lots of lovely times with them and we have many happy and sometimes humorous memories to look back on.

When the summer holiday time came, we started having families and various church groups coming for holidays or conferences, so it was a really busy time for us all. With them we had the pleasure of hosting some of the various leaders and elders of church fellowships, which was such a blessing to us. Norman Meeten came a few times, as did Mr North, John Simkin, John Norris, Peter Palmer and Ron Bailey to mention but a few. As well as this, Pete and Sue Moffat and Len Grates were fairly regular visitors with the Liverpool youth group for weekends.

Ann Didier

A French girl called Ann Diddier came to help us through

the summer months. She was a very sweet girl who often amused us when doing the hoovering by saying in her very French accent 'thee wyte beets won't go up my oover' – translation 'the white bits won't go up my hoover.' She also played the violin very nicely in the meetings and was a real blessing.

It was a busy summer and hard work for us staff in the house and I suppose you could ask why we wanted to do it. To my mind, I felt it was a privilege to minister to the local fellowship and also to those who visited. There were also times when some folk were able to come to us for a break or holiday who for various reasons would not be able to get away under normal circumstances.

I'm not sure how we managed all the catering that first summer, because while we had a food preparation room at the back of the house, we only had a small cooker and the Rayburn oven. In October I managed to find a second hand commercial electric cooker for sale on Anglesey, which we installed in the back kitchen which made such a big difference.

Another difficulty we faced was that we only had one set of nylon sheets for each of the beds, so at weekends when we had a changeover of folk leaving and coming we had to strip the beds, wash the sheets, tumble dry them and get them back on the beds before the next group came – phew! it was a busy time.

Early on we made an important addition to the house. We had noticed in the Cash and Carry that they sold boxes of chocolate bars and sweets, so we started a tuck shop. It became very popular with our visitors, but we couldn't resist using it ourselves too when it came to break times. Especially loved were the Toffee Crisp dark chocolate bars but when they were discontinued, Sue Lonergan wrote a humorous letter to Rowntree's to complain. She received a nice letter back from them apologizing, with four free milk chocolate Toffee Crisp bars to compensate for her disappointment!! Now why didn't I think of that!

Jenny

Moving to Bryn Goleu was quite an upheaval for our Jenny. Not only was she leaving her home, but also all her friends. Our flat in Liverpool was all on one level, and now we were living on the top floor of a big house, coming down two flights of stairs to the ground floor each day to have breakfast sitting round a big table with lots of other people.

There was a big garden to play in, and a swing to go on, but it was not much fun on her own. However, soon there was some companionship for her when many of our friends from Liverpool started coming with their children to spend a few days with us.

Jean's best friend Enid came with her children whom she'd played with such a lot in Liverpool, and as the summer brought more family and church groups, Jenny soon made many new friends, and would often be invited to join them on their days out in the local beauty spots. The picture shows Jenny and friend Stevie John Harrison from Liverpool.

Jenny also came with us when Jean and I went to do the weekly shop at the Cash and Carry.

Even though she was only three, she wanted to help us and would insist on pushing the trolley, which was long and hard to steer, up and down the aisles for us. (We had to keep an eye on her though, as she was not very good at stopping it if someone was ahead of us.)

Our first summer in Bryn Goleu was quite pleasant for us all in the house, as we seemed to have quite a few warm sunny days. Most guests went out for the day so we were able to get on with our normal routine. At lunchtimes we often ate out in the warm sunshine on the benches in the front garden, after which work would commence preparing for the evening meal.

My workload consisted of a lot of time in the gardens, mowing the lawns etc, and also office work, keeping up to date with the bookings diary and accounts. While the tuck shop was much appreciated by everyone, it also produced quite a lot of work for me, counting and bagging all the cash to be taken to the village HSBC bank. I was to become quite a regular customer there and they soon got to know me. The only trouble was they seemed to have great faith and trust in me, and mostly took my bags of coins and threw them into the drawer without counting it. This meant I felt I had to double check everything I took in, to make sure it was right.

I also had to spend time studying and preparing for the Sunday services, sometimes having to preach in both morning and evening meetings. I discovered though that I had a bit of a problem with my times in the office, as it was situated on the middle floor at the front of the house, giving me a superb view of the Llanfairfechan beach front with Anglesey and Puffin Island across the Menai Straights. I was fascinated with the tides and different states of the sea, sometimes so calm and other times windy and rough. I found it all so wonderful to sit and watch, and it became difficult to concentrate on what I was supposed to be doing. This problem was eventually solved in the autumn when we came up with the idea of moving the office up into one of the attic rooms, and we made the old office into a bedroom for Jan. That meant she slept nearer to Mam at night, and it gave Jean and I a bit more room at our end of the attic. My new office now only had a view of the mountain behind us, which was much less interesting.

Days off

Days off for us were a great opportunity to explore North Wales and Anglesey and we had some wonderful times with our little Jenny, which I guess was one of the perks of the job.

Trearddur Bay, Anglesey (we think)

Llandudno beach

Swallow Falls with my sister Grace, husband John and children

Ivan

One Sunday that summer, an elderly gentleman showed up for the meeting. He could speak very little English, so John and Sue explained to us that he was Russian and his name was Ivan; he lived in London but came every summer to camp in Penmaenmawr, and walked over to Bryn Goleu to come to all the meetings. Despite his English being very poor, we managed to communicate with him to some extent. One thing that stood out

Lunch in the garden, Ivan in the foreground

about him though was the way he prayed in the meetings. We may not have been able to understand any of it but could understand the passion and emotion he prayed with. He told us he prayed daily for the Queen and the government of UK, as they had accepted him after the 2nd World War when he was a refugee.

We soon became fond of him and invited him over quite often for lunch with us. He came every summer while we were there and sent us a Christmas card every year.

However, on the third Christmas we didn't hear from him, then a few months after Christmas a card came in the post with a letter included in it. It was from the landlady of the property where he lived and she explained that he had passed away over the Christmas period and as he had no one to sort out his stuff she had to go through it herself. In the process she came across a card addressed to us and had forwarded it to us. It was our Christmas card with a £20 note inside. We were very saddened and moved by it!

Autumn and winter 1979-80

When the summer ended we settled down to a more relaxed life-style. We still had visitors but on a level that was easier to manage and it was a pleasure to have them stay with us.

Jenny started going to the village school, which had its good points and difficulties. They did a lot of the teaching in Welsh in the time she was there, which was hard for her and also for the other children of English parents (of which there were a few), so from that point of view she didn't learn an awful lot.

She did however make several friends with girls in her class and started getting invited out after school for tea with them. On one occasion, she told us, the family all sat round the table and had begun to eat when Jenny said, 'Oh, you've forgotten to

say grace.' I think there must have been smiles all around the table as they explained to her they didn't say grace in their house.

As a result of Jenny going to school, we started getting to know people in the village and made some very lovely friends. Jenny also started having ballet lessons in the village hall which she really enjoyed.

Every year, there was a carnival procession in the village with lots of different floats coming down the roads, and in our second summer we were asked if Jenny could go on one of the floats. We didn't have a problem with that so agreed. Unknown to us, a lot of folk in the village were waiting to see if we would allow her to join in and I think it was another step forward to us being accepted among many.

One day that autumn I had to go over to the cottage for something and while there I found some of the children from the council estate in the back garden, scrumping from the apple trees. I told them they should not be doing this, but at the same time asked if they would like to have a Friday club in Bryn Goleu. They were interested, so together with John and Sue we started our children's club teaching them songs and choruses and Bible stories. It became a popular little club for these youngsters and we loved doing it with them. It continued in the Lonergans' cottage after we left Wales.

Sometime after this, we happened to meet Mrs 'Jones the Coal' in the launderette, and she mentioned that some of the teenagers in the area had nothing to do, and as a result were getting involved in drugs. There was growing concern from some in the village, she said, and they were asking if we would consider starting something for these young ones. Somehow, it came out that they called me Father Jim – I don't know how that came about. We said we would love to, but just then we were very busy in the work at Bryn Goleu. As it happened, we never managed to do anything about it, but Myrtle and Sue started a club for teenage girls at a later date after we had left.

Autumn and winter were very pleasant times for us. After breakfast, we took Jenny to school, and sometimes I took her in on a small motor bike that Jeff Clapham had given to us; Jenny really enjoyed that. I would pick up a paper while in the village and at break times we would all sit in the warm comfortable morning room, visit the tuck shop and sit round drinking our coffees, and I would have a bit of a read of the paper to keep me up to date with the goings on in the world (we didn't have a TV or radio in the house).

The winter evenings were restful too for us. If we had any guests, we would sit in the lounge (meeting room) and chat together while watching the amazing sunsets over Puffin Island. When we were on our own we'd often play board games with the others. On our days off, we would make our own evening meal in a little kitchenette which we had created in a small room in the attic, and enjoy the seclusion of our lovely lounge up there.

That autumn, Alwyn and Janet Griffiths, Lesley's uncle and aunt, wanted to come and join us, so they moved up from Stourbridge. They had sold their house with the intention of buying one in Llanfairfechan, but could not find a suitable one.

However, they located a plot of land just down the hill from us and bought that with the intention of building a bungalow on it. While building started, we let them stay in Bryn Goleu Lodge hoping they could move to their own home the following summer. The Lodge was a cottage opposite the end of Bryn Goleu drive; it made a great place for a family to have a self-contained holiday, as it had three bedrooms and its own lounge, kitchen and bathroom.

Through the winter Paul and I with the help of others set to work to make some alterations and improvements in the grounds. We figured that we needed more car parking space and started levelling some ground on the right of the driveway as you came in. We had to build a retaining wall around one side of it, so we had a go at dry stone walling, and I think we did quite a reasonable job! We needed some space for camping too, so we levelled the lawn behind the lodge to make room for a few tents. Paul then felt it would be good to remove some of the young trees from around the edge of the property. I think he felt it would open up the area so people could get a better view of the house and everything that took place here, and that this would dispel any thoughts by locals that something odd was going on there. We spent many hours of hard work on this, cutting down trees and digging up roots. It did also improve the view for us as well.

I think Paul got a bit carried away with this project though; in the spring he decided to prune the lovely rhododendron bush on the front lawn and he went a bit too far so there wasn't much of it left by the time he had finished. The following day we all said we hoped Mam wouldn't get out of bed to take a look at the garden. Wouldn't you just know it, it was a lovely sunny day and she decided to look out of the window so she saw what was left of the bush. She never made any comment!

As we finished our new car parking area, we cleared all the surrounding bushes to make a nice open space and made a big pile of the branches to have a bonfire. Before setting it alight we went in for our coffee break, but were startled shortly after by a loud boom. Running back to the car park we found Alwyn, who had been helping us, standing there looking a bit stunned. He had apparently thrown some petrol onto the bonfire to get it going, which had evaporated quickly and caused an explosion!

Fortunately, apart from some singed eyebrows he was unharmed. It gave him and us a good story to relate in years to come.

I had also discovered that winter that there was a problem with the fire in the lounge of the lodge; Alwyn had made a wood fire at times but when there were strong winds, it would cause a back draught and fill the room with smoke.

When spring came and Alwyn and Janet moved out for the summer, I thought if I changed the chimney pot with a special one that prevented the back draught it would probably solve the problem. So, one morning Jean and I set off for a builders yard in Bangor to buy a chimney pot.

On arrival, I left Jean in the car and went in. Now I should mention that in builders yards, they have technical names for lots of stuff that I don't know so I must have been feeling a bit nervous and when I went in through the front door I found myself in a little lobby with two more doors, I proceeded to go through the next door and seeing the counter ahead I went up to it and lent on it trying to look full of confidence.

After standing there for some time I started looking around, maybe there was a bell or something you rang to get service. Eventually I looked behind me and to my astonishment and horror there were lots of desks with men working at them. I was on the wrong side of the counter!!

I quickly retreated the way I had come in and felt even more like just making a run for it but plucked up courage and went in again through the other door where I was immediately served by a very pleasant gentleman who made no mention of my embarrassing mistake. I have to admit, though, I was pleased to get out with my purchase and go home.

Spiritual moral of the story – it's important to make sure you go through the right door in this life to be certain of future life in heaven. (See Matthew ch 7 v 13.)

Something else happened in that first winter in Wales: I made a chicken run up on the hill behind the house and bought six chickens, which I thought would be fun to have and also would give us a supply of eggs. The first egg went to Mam of course!

Around that time, our lovely Morris Traveller started having problems. Jeff Clapham kindly helped us at one point by putting a new radiator in it, but it continued to be in need of attention. The problem was resolved when we heard that the red VW van was back in Liverpool and nobody wanted it. It had a new engine but there was still a problem with the gear box. I decided to have a go at fixing it, and somehow we got it over to Wales and into John's garage in Pen', where we managed to fix the gearbox together – I think I gave the Morris to him, maybe as payment.

I liked to drop in quite often on John in the garage in Pen'; he was so kind and would help sort out car problems for us when they occurred. They also ran a coach hire service, which people from the Liverpool fellowship had used a few times for various events. After a while, the coach owner approached me to ask if I would like to learn to drive coaches. They would teach me and help me to get my PSV driver's licence in return for me doing the occasional bit of driving for them when they were short of a driver. It was a tempting offer, but after some consideration I turned it down because I felt it would put an extra workload on me and affect what I was really called to be doing at Bryn Goleu.

While we were living in Llanfairfechan, John from the garage died in some sad circumstances; I was very sorry, as I liked him very much and got on really well with him.

The VW was perfect for our needs with shopping etc, and I bought some wood panelling and managed to convert it from a van to a caravanette with bunk beds in the back for Jenny, while the passenger seats could be turned into a double bed. I was quite proud of my effort. The fact that it was a left-hand drive didn't seem to bother us, even on the narrow winding Welsh roads.

One more major event happened that winter: Jean found she was expecting our second child, Peter. This was wonderful for us and also good news for Jenny, as she had been praying she could have a brother. As with Jenny, Jean was quite sick for the first three months but only in the mornings.

One day in the spring, we were surprised when the mother of one Jenny's friends came up to see Jean, bringing some lovely Laura Ashley maternity dresses that she said she would not be needing again. We were very touched by the gift as we were sure she could have sold them very easily. We were also very touched after the birth of our next child when quite a few of the folk that we had come to know in the village bought us some lovely presents.

Summer 1980

Our next busy season began with a conference at the end of May with Pastor North as the speaker. I had to go down in the VW to collect him and his wife from Walsall, probably about a three-hour journey. I think he quite enjoyed the trip back sitting in the front with me, and Mrs North relaxed on the bench seat at the back of the van. This was still the time before it was compulsory to have seat belts in the back so she could stretch out and put her feet up.

The conference didn't start until the Monday, but Mr North wanted a rest before it, so he declined to speak to our small group on the Sunday. Instead, he sent his wife to listen to my preaching in the morning and evening and take back a report. His comment to me the following day was that she had enjoyed the meetings.

The conference week went well, then we had a welcome break of six weeks before the larger fellowship group holidays began.

In between, Jan Richardson became ill and was discovered to have appendicitis. In great pain, she had to be rushed to hospital in Bangor. Paul and Les were still with us so Les went with her in the ambulance with blue lights flashing. She returned a week later and had to rest and be looked after for a quite while afterwards.

We then had a week's holiday in Benllech Bay, Anglesey in a static caravan, which was lovely. We discovered that the beach mission people were there, so Jenny had a really enjoyable week with them, doing all the fun things they do and listening to the stories. We didn't have a lot of money but managed to buy Jenny an ice-cream every day.

After our holiday we started the summer season with Pete Moffat's youth group, a small conference with Edgar Parkins speaking, and then in the first week of August the Longcroft fellowship came for a week. This was the biggest group we had ever had with around 70 people. Somehow we crammed them all into the house and cottage, as well as some camping on the car park and in the cottage garden.

The week went well and we managed all the catering somehow. Each day after breakfast they prepared huge mounds of sandwiches to take out for their picnics and then they would be gone for the day, leaving us to clean the house and prepare for the evening meal.

One day Jean thought she would make some

ice cream for pudding using the Kenwood mixer. Unfortunately, during the process a nut fell off the machine into the bowl and disappeared into the mixture. It couldn't be found, that is, until someone found it in their sweet that evening when it was served. It caused some amusement, to the extent that on the Friday night when they had a concert, one of the songs was about Jeans 'nutty' ice cream.

Fortunately, we had a good team to get us through that busy summer, consisting of (from left) Astrid from Austria, me and Jean with Jenny, Jan Richardson, Mercia from Spain and Myrtle Jones

We had a few other groups that summer, till finally in September we settled back to a more

normal life, of just a few holiday visitors each week.

In the autumn, I had to take Jean to Bangor hospital each week to her antenatal appointments, and on 20th October she was admitted into hospital. Jean's mum and dad came over to look after Jenny. On the 21st our son Peter was born at 9.30 pm. In answer to our prayers, it was a normal birth.

On Friday 24th, I brought them both home in our VW caravanette on a beautiful sunny morning, with all the trees in their autumn glory. It was a lovely day for us, and Jenny was so pleased to have a little brother at last.

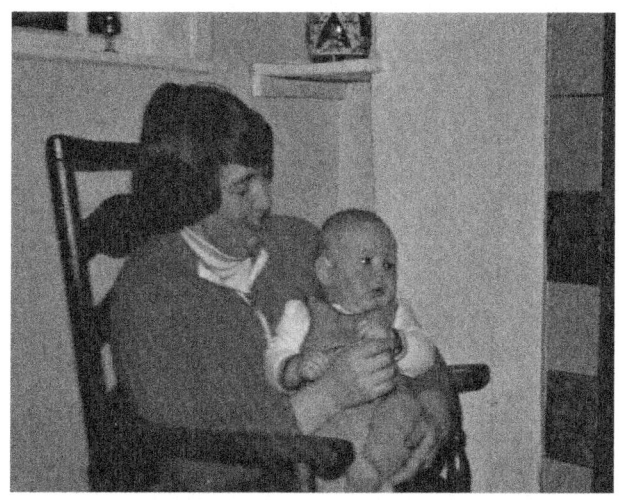

Peter proved to be a happy, hungry baby and soon settled into a good routine for us and slept well at night. I think after a few weeks Jean was able to be downstairs during the day and would feed him in the morning room sitting in Mam's favourite chair.

I think Jean did very well considering we were living in a communal situation but I don't think it was easy for her. We were still having visitors through the winter, and she wanted to be a part of the work so would often be helping with the washing up with Peter in a sling on her front.

Thankfully, around this time Paul Dawson came over from Liverpool to help us. He proved to be such a help to Jean with his banter and humour, and I think during this time he kept us both going. He was to become one of our best friends throughout our lives.

I asked him if he would take on looking after the hens for me which he did even though he hated the smell of them and showed it. He talked about 'going to feed the budgies' and pulled faces!

After a few months, Mam said to us she would like to buy something for Peter and we should go out to get whatever we needed and she would give us the money. We were at a point where we really needed a high chair for him, so on our next day off we paid a visit to Mothercare in Llandudno and bought one for around £20. On our return we brought our purchase up to show Mam. She thought it was lovely and just what we needed *but* unfortunately by this time she had forgotten her offer to us. (We never mentioned it to her!)

The work on Alwyn's bungalow was coming on well; the walls and windows were all done, then the roof went on, the electrics were in — and at that point they ran out of money. It was still not finished that summer, so they bought a small caravan and put it on their property and lived there for the summer so we could have the use of the cottage again. After the busy time was over, they moved back into the cottage for the autumn and winter.

Alwyn and Janet with their daughter Lisa (left) in their unfinished bungalow

In the autumn of 1980, John and Celia

Valentine came to stay with us for several weeks with their daughter Grace who must have been about one. It was such a pleasure to have them with us. In true Valentine style, John saw the problem Alwyn had with his bungalow and promptly offered our help to get the work going again.

The next job needed was to get all the inside walls rendered. Sand and cement was brought in and a cement mixer hired. John and I put 2x1 inch battens on the walls to get an even depth of plastering, then while Paul mixed the cement for us we got on with covering all the walls in the house. It was hard work and must have taken quite a few weeks. It was only towards the end we discovered that we could have put a much thinner coat on. Our joke afterwards, though, was that if the bricks in the walls were to fall out, the house would still be standing because of the strength of the rendering.

The Griffiths did eventually finish the house somehow, and it was a really lovely home for them with beautiful views and a nice garden. In later years we went to stay there for a week while they were away on holiday, which was kind of them.

As we approached spring of 1981, I think we were both quite tired but also Jean was not feeling very well. Peter had started crawling, then walking and would happily get into everything he could find. Sue Lonergan had a small book stall in the Bryn Goleu hallway with a quite a low bottom shelf and it was his joy to come along and sweep all the books off it. He wasn't being naughty, just full of life and energy.

Despite all this, we carried on as usual, and had some lovely times with our family coming to stay in April, then in June we started having various groups coming for a week at a time.

In the last week of July, Mr North came again for another conference, and while he was with us stopped to have a bit of a chat with us. I think he saw that we were not ourselves and he suggested we should have a break and a rest for a while, maybe for three months. Looking at the options, one suggestion was that we could go and live in Bryn Celyn, another big house just down the hill from us where a Christian lady lived who would have the space for us, and that Brian and Tegwen

Rainford should come and take over from us for the time being.

We carried on through the busy summer period and in the end decided we would prefer to go back home to Liverpool for our break. I didn't record the actual date we left but think it was probably around early October.

Brian and Tegwen came to live and take over from us, and we packed up all the clothes we were going to need into our caravanette. In saying goodbye to MamBailey, she said to me 'You won't be coming back, will you.' I was quite surprised by this comment, and hoped it wasn't prophetic.

We waved goodbye to our friends there that afternoon heading back to Liverpool, not really knowing what our future was to be, but God had a plan and a purpose which over the coming weeks we were to find out.

More to come in part two.

Printed in Great Britain
by Amazon